1st EDITION

Perspectives on Diseases and Disorders

Autoimmune Diseases

Jacqueline Langwith
Book Editor

PERSPECTIVES
On Diseases & Disorders

GALE
CENGAGE Learning™

Detroit • New York • San Francisco • New Haven, Conn • Waterville, Maine • London

Christine Nasso, *Publisher*
Elizabeth Des Chenes, *Managing Editor*

© 2011 Greenhaven Press, a part of Gale, Cengage Learning

Gale and Greenhaven Press are registered trademarks used herein under license.

For more information, contact:
Greenhaven Press
27500 Drake Rd.
Farmington Hills, MI 48331-3535
Or you can visit our Internet site at gale.cengage.com

For product information and technology assistance, contact us at

Gale Customer Support, 1-800-877-4253
For permission to use material from this text or product, submit all requests online at
www.cengage.com/permissions

Further permissions questions can be e-mailed to permissionrequest@cengage.com

Articles in Greenhaven Press anthologies are often edited for length to meet page requirements. In addition, original titles of these works are changed to clearly present the main thesis and to explicitly indicate the author's opinion. Every effort is made to ensure that Greenhaven Press accurately reflects the original intent of the authors. Every effort has been made to trace the owners of copyrighted material.

Cover image © Science Photo Library/Alamy

LIBRARY OF CONGRESS CATALOGING-IN-PUBLICATION DATA

Autoimmune diseases / Jacqueline Langwith, book editor.
   p. cm. -- (Perspectives on diseases and disorders)
 Includes bibliographical references and index.
 ISBN 978-0-7377-5251-9 (hardcover)
 1. Autoimmune diseases. I. Langwith, Jacqueline.
 RC600.A8312 2011
 616.97'8--dc22

                           2011000939

Printed in the United States of America
1 2 3 4 5 6 7 15 14 13 12 11

CONTENTS

CHAPTER 1   Understanding Autoimmune Diseases

Monique Laberge and Tish Davidson

There are more than eighty different autoimmune diseases, characterized by the involvement of an inappropriate immune response that leads the body to attack its own cells and tissues.

National Institue of Allergy and Infectious Diseases

The immune system comprises a variety of components, including a number of specialized organs and cells. Some of the most essential elements are the thymus, lymph nodes, and B and T cells.

Noel R. Rose

Autoimmune diseases all have one element in common—autoimmunity. While the causes of autoimmunity have not yet been established, genetics and environment are both known to play a role.

FOREWORD

"Medicine, to produce health, has to examine disease."
—Plutarch

Independent research on a health issue is often the first step to complement discussions with a physician. But locating accurate, well-organized, understandable medical information can be a challenge. A simple Internet search on terms such as "cancer" or "diabetes," for example, returns an intimidating number of results. Sifting through the results can be daunting, particularly when some of the information is inconsistent or even contradictory. The Greenhaven Press series Perspectives on Diseases and Disorders offers a solution to the often overwhelming nature of researching diseases and disorders.

From the clinical to the personal, titles in the Perspectives on Diseases and Disorders series provide students and other researchers with authoritative, accessible information in unique anthologies that include basic information about the disease or disorder, controversial aspects of diagnosis and treatment, and first-person accounts of those impacted by the disease. The result is a well-rounded combination of primary and secondary sources that, together, provide the reader with a better understanding of the disease or disorder.

Each volume in Perspectives on Diseases and Disorders explores a particular disease or disorder in detail. Material for each volume is carefully selected from a wide range of sources, including encyclopedias, journals, newspapers, nonfiction books, speeches, government documents, pamphlets, organization newsletters, and position papers. Articles in the first chapter provide an authoritative, up-to-date overview that covers symptoms, causes and effects, treatments, cures, and medical advances. The second chapter presents a substantial number of opposing viewpoints on controversial treatments and other current debates relating to the volume topic. The third chapter offers a variety of personal perspectives on the disease or disorder. Patients, doctors, caregivers, and loved ones represent just some of the voices found in this narrative chapter.

Each Perspectives on Diseases and Disorders volume also includes:

- An **annotated table of contents** that provides a brief summary of each article in the volume.
- An **introduction** specific to the volume topic.
- Full-color **charts and graphs** to illustrate key points, concepts, and theories.
- Full-color **photos** that show aspects of the disease or disorder and enhance textual material.
- **"Fast Facts"** that highlight pertinent additional statistics and surprising points.
- A **glossary** providing users with definitions of important terms.
- A **chronology** of important dates relating to the disease or disorder.
- An annotated list of **organizations to contact** for students and other readers seeking additional information.
- A **bibliography** of additional books and periodicals for further research.
- A detailed **subject index** that allows readers to quickly find the information they need.

Whether a student researching a disorder, a patient recently diagnosed with a disease, or an individual who simply wants to learn more about a particular disease or disorder, a reader who turns to Perspectives on Diseases and Disorders will find a wealth of information in each volume that offers not only basic information, but also vigorous debate from multiple perspectives.

INTRODUCTION

When people think of an immune system, they generally think of the incredibly complex immune system of humans and other mammals. But insects, fish, other animals, and plants also have immune systems. The capacity to detect cellular threats and neutralize them has been essential for survival since the earliest days of life. Even simple unicellular organisms such as bacteria possess mechanisms to ward off viral intruders. Two different types of immune systems exist in nature: an ancient "innate" immune system and a more advanced "adaptive" immune system.

The functions of both types of immune systems are to detect invading cells or substances and then destroy them. The innate system carries out these functions in a general way. It recognizes foreign substances, although it does not distinguish between them. Once any type of foreign substance is detected, the innate immune system mobilizes a standing army of toxic molecules, which are ready to do battle at a moment's notice. The adaptive immune system, on the other hand, is more specific and slower acting. It distinguishes between different types of foreign substances and then develops, over periods of days to weeks, an army designed specifically against each one.

The innate immune system is an evolutionarily older defense strategy. Scientists think it arose roughly 1 billion years ago in single-celled life forms. It is theorized that ancient life forms developed the ability to detect threats by first needing to identify food. The ability to destroy threats is speculated to have arisen by the harnessing of toxic proteins and other substances. The late Yale professor Charles A. Janeway, a preeminent immunologist and the author of the classic textbook *Immunology*, describes how the detection function of innate immunity may have arisen in the primitive single-celled amoeba. According to Janeway:

> Innate immunity . . . can be thought of as arising from the need of a unicellular microorganism such as an amoeba to discriminate between food and other amoebas. If you think about it, any amoeba that could not make this distinction would be bound to consume itself and vanish from the face of the Earth. Therefore, we can infer a specific surface receptor on amoebas that acts to discriminate between food, which can eagerly be engulfed, from what is another amoeba, or even another part of the same amoeba.[1]

Today the innate immune system is found throughout nature. It is the predominant form of protection in plants, fungi, and insects. In most animals, including humans, the innate immune system provides the first line of defense against invading organisms, while the more advanced adaptive immune system acts as a second line of defense.

The adaptive immune system is based on the concept of "immunological memory." In adaptive immunity, special cells, called T cells and B cells, encounter an invader, learn how to attack it, and remember the specific invader so that they can attack it even more efficiently the next time they encounter it. Specific immunity takes from two days to two weeks to develop, since the immune cells must adapt to the new invader.

The effectiveness of vaccination is based on the immunological memory of the adaptive immune system. Antibodies, which are made from B cells, are a major component of the adaptive immune system. Vaccines usually expose a person to a killed or weakened form of a disease-causing microbe, triggering the adaptive immune system to create antibodies. These antibodies circulate in the blood, and if the person is exposed to the microbe again, they attack it and neutralize it.

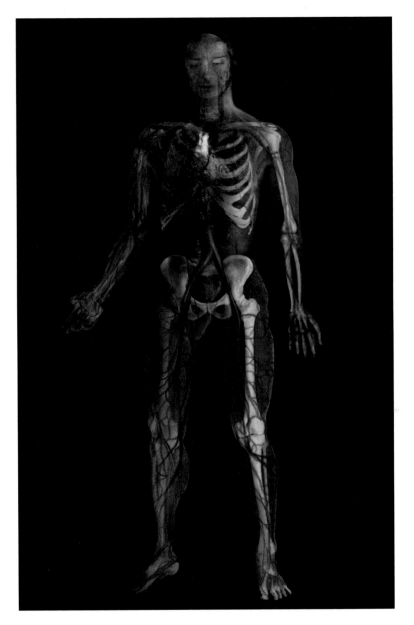

The immune system guards against invading organisms that cause infection and diseases. The innate system is made up of of chemical and mechanical barriers, such as skin and mucous membranes, that protect the body from invaders. The adaptive system is composed of white blood cells, which circulate in the blood and destroy microorganisms that have penetrated the chemical and mechanical barriers. **(Anatomical Travelogue/ Photo Researchers, Inc.)**

While the innate immune system is ancient and is common to all plants and animals, the adaptive immune system has been around for about half the amount of time and is only found in vertebrate animals—that is, those animals with a spine. Scientists believe a single genetic event occurring about 450 million years ago gave humans and other jawed animals the ability to respond to specific foreign invaders. It is hypothesized that at some point after jawed vertebrates split off from jawless vertebrates, a virus carrying a "jumping gene," called a transposon, invaded a fishlike member of the jawed lineage. It is thought that the transposon carried with it the genetic material that ultimately ended up producing T cells, B cells, and other components of the adaptive immune system.

The scientific evidence supporting this "big bang" event in the evolution of immunity was garnered over a period of many years in the latter part of the twentieth century. In the late 1970s, Massachusetts Institute of Technology professor Susumu Tonegawa showed how B cells could make an infinite number of different antibodies. In the 1990s David Schatz and other scientists working at the Whitehead Institute for Biomedical Research found that Tonegawa's antibody-producing mechanism was linked to two genes. These genes were found in all jawed vertebrates but were absent in hagfish and sea lampreys—the only surviving members of the jawless vertebrates. Then in the late 1990s, Schatz, Craig Thompson, and others found evidence showing that the two genes were originally derived from a transposon. In the August 1998 issue of the journal *Nature*, Dutch scientist Ronald Plasterk discussed the significance of these findings and the nature of transposons in his introduction to an article written by Schatz:

> Transposons are generally considered the ultimate forms of selfish DNA—a single gene (or sometimes a set of two or three genes) that spreads simply because it ensures its own replication. . . . But selfish elements may also end up doing something useful for their host, and it has often been speculated that transposon jumping may have generated gene arrangements that opened new avenues in evolution. Examples of this are rare, but a spectacular

case has now been discovered. David Schatz and his colleagues report that we owe the repertoire of our immune system to one transposon insertion, which occurred 450 million years ago in an ancestor of the jawed vertebrates.[2]

The research by Schatz and the other scientists, which revealed the evolution of the immune system, played a leading role in the controversy surrounding the teaching of intelligent design (ID) in US schools. In 2005 a group of parents in Dover, Pennsylvania, challenged the school district's decision to teach ID—which purports that humans did not evolve from other animals but were created—in the school district's biology classes. In the trial, ID proponent and biochemist Michael Behe asserted that there was inadequate proof to show that the human immune system evolved, and that its complexity necessitated the input of an intelligent creator. The trial went on for six weeks and included extensive expert testimony and in-depth evidence of the transposon event. When it was over, the judge in the case ruled in favor of those opposing the teaching of ID in schools. According to the judge, the evidence proves that, despite its incredible complexity, the human immune system evolved from ancient creatures and events.

The complexity of the immune system becomes apparent when one considers the number of different autoimmune diseases that exist. According to the American Autoimmune Related Diseases Association, there are more than one hundred serious, chronic autoimmune diseases. These diseases cause a wide range of symptoms, from the seemingly benign, such as hair loss or dry mouth, to the incapacitating and life-threatening difficulties associated with multiple sclerosis, diabetes, and rheumatoid arthritis. *In Perspectives on Diseases and Disorders: Autoimmune Diseases*, the contributors explain the science behind autoimmune diseases, debate controversial issues, and provide insight into the lives of those affected by these diseases.

Notes

1. Charles A. Janeway Jr., Paul Travers, Mark Walport, and Mark J. Shlomchik, *Immunology*, 5th ed. New York: Garland Science, 2001.
2. Ronald Plasterk, "V (D)J Recombination: Ragtime Jumping," *Nature*, August 20, 1998.

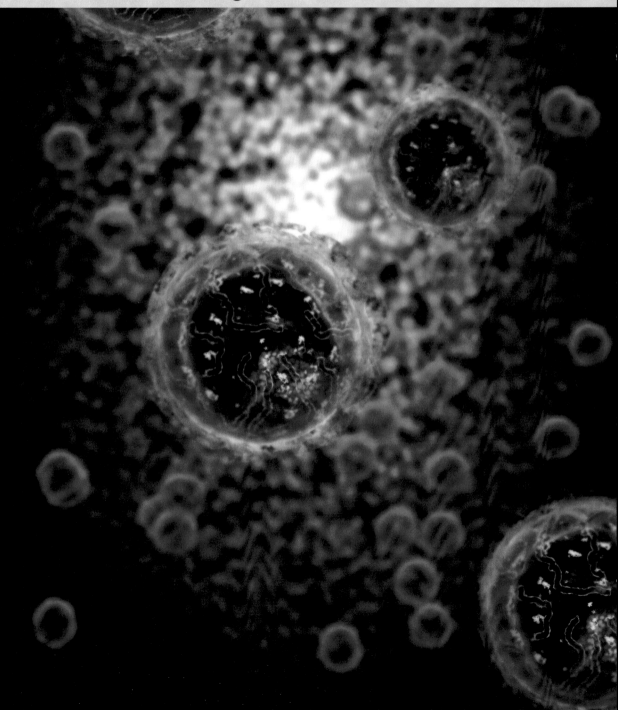

Understanding Autoimmune Diseases

An Overview of Autoimmune Diseases

Monique Laberge and Tish Davidson

In the following viewpoint Monique Laberge and Tish Davidson provide an overview of autoimmune diseases, a family of related diseases characterized by an immune system that turns on itself. According to Laberge and Davidson, there are more than eighty different types of autoimmune diseases; some affect the entire body, while others are tissue specific. Scientists do not fully understand why, but many of these disorders disproportionately affect women. The authors say that diagnosing and treating autoimmune disorders is difficult. There is no cure for autoimmune diseases yet, because scientists are still trying to understand the cause of these disorders. As a result, treatments are meant only to alleviate symptoms. Laberge is a physical chemist, and Davidson is a nationally recognized medical writer.

A ccording to a 2005 report by the National Institutes of Health (NIH), many specific autoimmune disorders are rare, meaning that they affect less than

Photo on previous page. A microscopic view of a B cell lymphocyte. B and T cells recognize and attack specific antigens, and some remain in the body to provide "memory" cells for the immune system to fight the pathogens more effectively if they return. (3D4Medical/ Photo Researchers, Inc.)

SOURCE: Monique Laberge and Tish Davidson, "Autoimmune Disorders," *Gale Encyclopedia of Medicine*, 3rd ed., Jacqueline L. Longe, ed. Copyright © 2009 Gale, a part of Cengage Learning, Inc. Reproduced by permission.

200,000 people. Nevertheless, collectively, these diseases afflict about 8% of the population of the United States. These disorders disproportionately affect women, and, for reasons that cannot yet be explained, their prevalence is rising.

For some disorders, such as scleroderma, systemic lupus erythematosus (SLE), and Sjögren's syndrome, more than 85% of patients are female. This gender disparity, although smaller, is still observed in other autoimmnne disorders, such as multiple sclerosis and inflammatory bowel disease. A few diseases, such as type 1 diabetes, affect men and women almost equally. The reasons for the gender disparity are not well understood, but the production of sex hormones is now thought to represent an important factor.

Americans of African origin seem to be at higher risk than Americans of European origin for SLE and scleroderma, but are at lower risk for type 1 diabetes (formerly called juvenile diabetes) and multiple sclerosis. High rates of certain autoimmune diseases have also been reported in specific Native American groups. Asian Americans living in Hawaii have some of the lowest rates reported for multiple sclerosis and type 1 diabetes, but these rates seem to increase in those who move to the United States mainland.

Autoimmunity is accepted as the cause of a wide range of disorders, and it is suspected to be responsible for many more. Autoimmune diseases are classified as either general (systemic), in which the autoimmune reaction takes place simultaneously in a number of tissues, or organ specific, in which the autoimmune reaction targets a single organ. Individuals may, and often do, have more than one autoimmune disorder.

The Immune System

The immune system consists of the organs and cells of the lymphatic system that protect the body against infections and other diseases. It is the body's defense mechanism against foreign invaders such as harmful microorganisms (pathogens). The sum of the defensive reactions triggered by the presence of a foreign substance or organism in the body is called an immune response. A foreign substance that can trigger an immune response is called an antigen.

The main cells involved in an immune response are white blood cells (leukocytes) called lymphocytes. There are two types of lymphocytes—B lymphocytes (B cells) and T lymphocytes (T cells)—that can recognize antigens. The mechanism by which these cells recognize and attack specific antigens is called adaptive immunity, because after the first response of lymphocytes to a pathogen, some of the B and T cells remain and provide "memory" cells for the immune system to fight the pathogen more effectively when it comes back. The B lymphocytes mature in the bone marrow and produce antibodies, specialized proteins that can attack antigens and help the body destroy them. Antibodies are also called immunoglobulins (Ig), of which there are five main classes: IgA, IgD, IgE, IgG, and IgM. IgG and IgM are the antibodies that protect against infectious diseases. The T lymphocytes mature in the thymus and help B cells to make antibodies. T lymphocytes can attack virus-infected cells and antigens directly.

At birth, an infant only has antibodies that are transferred through the placenta from the mother (a condition called passive immunity). Maternal antibodies gradually disappear during the first 6–8 months of life. Infants begin to make their own antibodies at an increased rate soon after birth in response to antigenic stimulation by antigens in the environment. As a child grows, so does its immune system complement: protective T lymphocytes and new antibodies produced after exposure to specific antigens. The immune system undergoes continuous changes throughout life. It reaches its peak function at puberty and gradually starts to deteriorate with advancing age (immunosenescence).

In a healthy person, the immune system can distinguish between its own cells and tissues and those that represent foreign threats. Autoimmune disorders are the result of a breakdown in this recognition system, allowing the body to produce an immune response against itself, called an autoimmune response. This triggers the production of autoantibodies that attack the body's own cells, tissues, or organs.

Types of Autoimmune Disorders

There are more than 80 chronic and often disabling types of autoimmune disorders. Well known disorders include rheumatoid arthritis, multiple sclerosis, type 1 diabetes, celiac disease, and SLE. Other less known disorders include autoimmune hemolytic anemia and Sjögren's syndrome. Examples of autoimmune disorders are:

- Amyotrophic lateral sclerosis. Also called Lou Gehrig's disease. An immune disorder that causes the death of neurons, which leads to progressive loss of muscular control.
- Ankylosing spondylitis. Immune system induced degeneration of the joints and soft tissue of the spine.
- Autoimmune hemolytic anemia. Occurs when the body produces antibodies that target red blood cells.
- Autoimmune thrombocytopenic purpura. A disorder in which the immune system targets and destroys blood platelets.
- Celiac disease (sprue). A disease in which the body's reaction to gluten (most commonly found in wheat) causes damage to the intestines that results in poor absorption of nutrients.
- Goodpasture's syndrome. Occurs when antibodies are deposited in the membranes of both the lungs and kidneys, causing both inflammation of kidney glomerulus (glomerulonephritis) and lung bleeding. It is typically a disease of young males.

Autoimmune Diseases Affect Many Organs and Organ Systems

Autoimmune

Nervous System:

Multiple sclerosis

Myasthenia gravis

Autoimmune neuropathies, such as Guillain-Barré

Autoimmune uveitis

Blood:

Autoimmune hemolytic anemia

Pernicious anemia

Autoimmune thrombocytopenia

Blood Vessels:

Temporal arteritis

Antiphospholipid syndrome

Vasculitides such as Wegener's granulomatosis

Behcet's disease

Skin:

Psoriasis

Dermatitis herpetiformis

Pemphigus vulgaris

Vitiligo

Gastrointestinal System:

Crohn's disease

Ulcerative colitis

Primary biliary cirrhosis

Autoimmune hepatitis

Endocrine Glands:

Type 1 or immune-mediated diabetes mellitus

Graves' disease

Hashimoto's thyroiditis

Autoimmune oophoritis and orchitis

Autoimmune disease of the adrenal gland

Multiple Organs, Including the Musculoskeletal System:

Rheumatoid arthritis

Systemic lupus erythematosus

Scleroderma

Polymyositis, dermatomyositis

Spondyloarthropathies, such as ankylosing spondylitis

Sjögren's syndrome

- Graves' disease. Caused by an antibody that binds to specific cells in the thyroid gland causing them to produce excessive amounts of thyroid hormone.
- Guillain-Barre syndrome. Also called infectious polyneuritis. A rare disorder that sometimes occurs after an infection or an immunization, Guillain-Barre syndrome affects the myelin sheath that covers nerve cells. It causes progressive muscle weakness and paralysis.
- Hashimoto's thyroiditis. Caused by an antibody that binds to cells in the thyroid gland. Unlike Graves' disease, this antibody's action results in less thyroid hormone being producing.
- Multiple sclerosis. An autoimmune disorder that may involve a virus, it affects the central nervous system causing loss of coordination and muscle control.
- Myasthenia gravis. A condition in which the immune system attacks a receptor on the surface of muscle cells, preventing the muscle from receiving nerve impulses and resulting in severe muscle weakness.
- Pemphigus vulgaris. A group of autoimmune disorders that affect the skin.
- Pernicious anemia. Disorder in which the immune system attacks the lining of the stomach in such a way that the body cannot metabolize vitamin B_{12}.
- Polymyositis and dermatomyositis. Immune disorders that affect the neuromuscular system.
- Rheumatoid arthritis. Occurs when the immune system attacks and destroys the tissues that line bone joints and cartilage. The disease occurs throughout the body, although some joints may be more affected than others.
- Scleroderma. Also called CREST syndrome or progressive systemic sclerosis, scleroderma affects the connective tissue.

- Sjögren's syndrome. Occurs when the exocrine glands are attacked by the immune system, resulting in excessive dryness.
- Systemic lupus erythematosus. A general autoimmune disease in which antibodies attack a number of different tissues. The disease recurs periodically and is seen mainly in young and middle-aged women.
- Type 1 diabetes mellitus. Appears to be caused by an antibody that attacks and destroys the islet cells of the pancreas, which produce insulin.
- Vasculitis. A group of autoimmune disorders in which the immune system attacks and destroys blood vessels.

No Known Cause

The cause or causes of autoimmune disorders is unknown, but all these disorders result from malfunctions of the mechanisms that regulate immune system function. The purpose of the immune system is to defend the body against attack by infectious microbes (e.g., bacteria, viruses, fungi) and foreign materials (e.g., chemicals, poisons). When the immune system attacks a foreign invader, it is very specific—a particular immune system cell will only recognize and target one type of invader. To function properly, the immune system must not only develop this specialized knowledge of individual invaders, but it must also learn how to recognize and not destroy cells that belong to the body itself.

Every cell carries protein markers on its surface that identify it in one of two ways: what kind of cell it is (e.g., nerve cell, muscle cell, blood cell, etc.) and to whom that cell belongs. These markers are called major histocompatability complexes (MHCs). When functioning properly, cells of the immune system will not attack any cell with markers identifying it as belonging to the body. Conversely, if the immune system cells do not recognize a cell as "self," they attach themselves to it and put out a signal that the body has been invaded. This stimulates the production of substances such as antibodies that disable and destroy the foreign particles. In the case of autoimmune disorders, the immune system cannot distinguish between "self" cells and invader cells. As a result, the same destructive operation is carried out on the body's own cells that would normally be carried out on bacteria, viruses, and other harmful foreign materials.

The reasons why immune systems become dysfunctional and fail to recognize the body's own cells is not well understood. Most researchers agree that a combination of genetic susceptibility, environmental, and hormonal factors play a role in developing autoimmunity. Researchers also hypothesize that autoimmunity may be triggered by several different mechanisms as follows:

- A substance that is normally sequestered in one part of the body, and, therefore, not usually exposed to the immune system, is released into the bloodstream where it is attacked.
- The immune system may mistake a component of the body for a similar foreign component.
- Cells of the body may be altered in some way, either by drugs, infection, or other environmental factors, so that they are no longer recognizable as "self" to the immune system.
- The immune system itself may be damaged, such as by a genetic mutation, and becomes dysfunctional.

Autoimmune Diseases Share Symptoms

Many autoimmune diseases share similar symptoms, and many symptoms are not specific to these disorders. A short summary of symptoms is as follows:

- Systemic lupus erythematosus. Symptoms include fever, chills, fatigue, weight loss, skin rashes (particularly the classic "butterfly" rash on the face), vasculitis, polyarthralgia, patchy hair loss, sores in the mouth or nose, lymph-node enlargement, gastric problems, and, in women, irregular periods. About half of those who experience lupus develop cardiopulmonary problems, and some may develop urinary problems. Lupus can also affect the central nervous system, causing seizures, depression, and psychosis.

- Rheumatoid arthritis. Initially, this disorder may be characterized by a low-grade fever, loss of appetite, weight loss, and generalized pain in the joints. The joint pain becomes more specific, usually beginning in the fingers, then spreading to other areas, such as the wrists, elbows, knees, and ankles. As the disease progresses, joint function diminishes sharply and deformities occur, particularly the characteristic "swan's neck" curling of the fingers.
- Goodpasture's syndrome. Symptoms are similar to that of iron deficiency anemia, including fatigue and pallor. Symptoms involving the lungs may range from a cough that produces bloody sputum to outright hemorrhaging. Symptoms involving the urinary system include blood in the urine and/or swelling.
- Graves' disease. This disease is characterized by an enlarged thyroid gland, weight loss without loss of appetite, sweating, heart palpitations, nervousness, and an inability to tolerate heat.
- Hashimoto's thyroiditis. This disorder generally displays few symptoms.
- Pemphigus vulgaris. Characteristic symptoms are blisters and deep lesions on the skin.
- Myasthenia gravis. Characterized by fatigue and muscle weakness that at first may be confined to certain muscle groups, but then may progress to the point of paralysis. Myasthenia gravis patients often have expressionless faces as well as difficulty chewing and swallowing. If the disease progresses to the

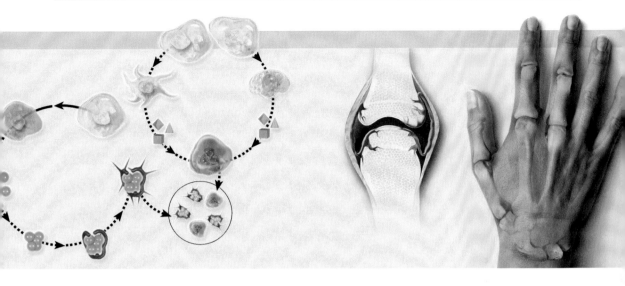

respiratory system, artificial respiration may be required.

- Scleroderma. This disorder usually is preceded by Raynaud's phenomenon [blood vessel constriction, typically in fingers and toes]. Symptoms that follow include pain, swelling, and stiffness of the joints, and the skin takes on a tight, shiny appearance. The digestive system becomes involved resulting in weight loss, appetite loss, diarrhea, constipation, and distention of the abdomen. As the disease progresses, the heart, lungs, and kidneys become involved, and malignant hypertension (high blood pressure) causes death in approximately 30% of cases.

- Autoimmune hemolytic anemia. May be acute or chronic. Symptoms include fatigue and abdominal tenderness due to an enlarged spleen.

- Autoimmune thrombocytopenic purpura. Characterized by pinhead-size red dots on the skin, unexplained bruises, bleeding from the nose and gums, and blood in the stool.

- Polymyositis and dermatomyositis. In polymyositis, symptoms include muscle weakness, particularly in the shoulders or pelvis, which prevents the patient

This illustration shows various aspects of rheumatoid arthritis. At left, two sets of cellular mechanisms show B cells (green), a plasma cell (brown), a macrophage (yellow, with protrusions), an osteoclast (orange), and a T cell (blue). The cutaway art at the left of the hand shows a single knuckle joint with arthritis. The hand has bone and joint anatomy superimposed, showing swelling around the knuckles and wristbones caused by the cellular processes outlined on the left. (Claus Lunau/ Bonier Publications/ Photo Researchers, Inc.)

from performing everyday activities. In dermato-myositis, the same muscle weakness is accompanied by a rash on the upper body, arms, and fingertips. A rash may also appear on the eyelids, and the area around the eyes may become swollen.

- Pernicious anemia. Signs of pernicious anemia include weakness, sore tongue, bleeding gums, and tingling in the extremities. A decrease in stomach acid results in possible nausea, vomiting, loss of appetite, weight loss, diarrhea, and constipation. A deficiency of vitamin B_{12}, which is essential for the nervous system function, is brought about by the disease and can result in a host of neurological problems, including weakness, lack of coordination, blurred vision, loss of fine motor skills, loss of the sense of taste, ringing in the ears, and loss of bladder control.
- Sjögren's syndrome. Characterized by excessive dryness of the mouth and eyes.
- Ankylosing spondylitis. Generally begins with lower back pain that progresses up the spine. The pain may eventually become crippling.
- Vasculitis. Symptoms depend upon the group of veins affected and can vary greatly.
- Type 1 diabetes mellitus. Characterized by fatigue and the inability to break down glucose, resulting in an abnormally high level of glucose in the blood (hyperglycemia).
- Amyotrophic lateral sclerosis. First signs are stumbling and difficulty climbing stairs. Later, muscle cramps and twitching may be observed as well as weakness in the hands that makes fastening buttons or turning a key difficult. Speech may become slowed or slurred. There may also be difficulty swallowing. As respiratory muscles atrophy, there is increased danger of aspiration or lung infection.
- Guillain-Barré syndrome. Muscle weakness in the legs occurs first, then the arms and face. Paresthesia

is often present. This disorder affects both sides of the body and may involve paralysis of the muscles that control breathing.

• Multiple sclerosis. Like amyotrophic lateral sclerosis, the first symptom may be clumsiness. Weakness or exhaustion is often reported, as is blurry or double vision. The individual may experience dizziness, depression, loss of bladder control, and muscle weakness so severe that the patient is confined to a wheelchair.

• Celiac disease. Damage to the lining of the small intestine causes immediate difficulties in digesting food resulting in diarrhea, gas, and cramps; and long-term symptoms of vitamin and mineral deficiencies such as anemia, osteoporosis, and weight loss. . . . .

Diagnosis Is Difficult

Due to numerous types of autoimmune disorders, diagnosis is often hard to establish. Another difficulty is that the symptoms of many autoimmune disorders, such as fatigue or diarrhea, also occur in other diseases. It also happens that a person may have more than one autoimmune disease. For instance, patients with Addison's disease often have type 1 diabetes as well. Giant cell arteritis is found in approximately 50% of patients with polymyalgia. A detailed history of symptoms and a complete physical examination are essential to start establishing diagnosis.

A variety of tests are involved in the diagnosis of autoimmune disorders depending on the particular disease such as blood tests, cerebrospinal fluid analysis, electromyogram (measures muscle function), and magnetic resonance imaging (MRI) of the brain. Usually, these tests determine the location and extent of damage or involvement. They also are useful in charting progress of the disease and as baselines for treatment.

The principle tool for authenticating autoimmune disease is antibody testing. These tests measure the level of antibodies found in the blood and determine if they react with specific antigens that would give rise to an autoimmune reaction. An elevated amount of antibodies indicates that a general immune reaction is occurring. Since elevated antibody levels are seen in common infections, infections must be ruled out as the cause for the increased antibody levels.

Antibodies can be typed by class. There are five classes of antibodies, and they can be separated in the laboratory. The class IgG is usually associated with autoimmune diseases. Unfortunately, IgG class antibodies are also the main class of antibody seen in normal immune responses.

The most useful antibody tests involve introducing the patient's antibodies to samples of his or her own tissue, usually thyroid, stomach, liver, and kidney tissue. If antibodies bind to the "self" tissue, this is diagnostic for an autoimmune disorder. Antibodies from a person without an autoimmune disorder would not react to "self" tissue.

Treatment to Alleviate Symptoms

Treatment of autoimmune diseases is specific to the disease and typically focuses on alleviating or preventing symptoms rather than correcting the underlying cause. For example, if a gland involved in an autoimmune reaction is not producing a hormone (e.g., insulin), administration of that hormone is required. Administration of a hormone, however, will not restore the function of the gland damaged by the autoimmune disease.

The other aspect of treatment is controlling the inflammatory and proliferative nature of the immune response. This is accomplished with two types of drugs. Corticosteroid compounds (e.g., prednisone) are used to control inflammation. There are many different corticosteroids, each having undesirable side effects, especially with long-term use. The current goal for patients with autoimmune disorders is to find treatments that relieve symptoms and/or produce remissions with the fewest side effects.

The proliferative nature of the immune response is controlled with immunosuppressive drugs (e.g., azathioprine, chlorambucil, cyclophosphamide, methotrexate). These drugs inhibit the replication of cells and suppress non-immune cells, leading to side effects such as anemia (too few red blood cells). In addition, other drugs may be used to treat symptoms of specific disorders.

Another approach is the use of drugs such as entanercept (Enbrel), imflixmab (Remicade), and adalimumab (Humira) that block the action of tumor necrosis factor (TNF). TNF is a substance that can cause inflammation in the body. These drugs have proved very effective in relieving symptoms in people with rheumatoid arthritis. However, in June 2008, the U.S. Food and Drug Administration (FDA) began investigating whether these drugs, especially when administered long term to younger patients, caused an increase in cancer, especially lymphoma (cancer of the lymph tissue). As of 2009, the data on potential cancer risks related to these drugs was confusing and difficult to assess because many patients who developed cancer were taking other drugs in addition to TNFs.

Autoimmune research has started investigating nutritional factors that affect immune function and interactions between dietary factors and other exposures. For example, reports suggest that antioxidants may play a role in immune function, particularly with respect to autoimmunity. Lupus-prone mice have shown delayed symptom onset or prolonged survival when given antioxidant supplements. The potential role of diet in autoimmune disorders is emerging as an important issue for patients.

> **FAST FACT**
>
> The National Institutes of Health estimates that up to 23.5 million Americans suffer from an autoimmune disease and that the prevalence of such diseases is rising.

Prognosis and Prevention

Prognosis depends upon the pathology of each specific autoimmune disease. As of mid-2009, autoimmune disorders cannot be cured with treatment, although in rare cases they may disappear on their own. Many people experience flare-ups and temporary remissions in symptoms, others have chronic symptoms or a progressive worsening. Since cures are not yet available, patients are often faced with a lifetime of illness and treatment. They frequently endure debilitating symptoms, loss of organ function, and reduced productivity at work. Since the course the disorders take is unpredictable, it is very difficult for medical practitioners to foresee what will happen to the patient based on onset symptoms. However, many patients are able to live normal lives if their disorder can be medically managed. . . .

Since the cause of autoimmune disorders is not understood, they cannot be prevented. Increasing knowledge about the genetic and environmental factors contributing to these disorders carries the hope of developing effective prevention strategies to arrest the autoimmune process before it can irreversibly damage the body. A major goal of autoimmune disease research is to identify people at risk before irreversible organ damage occurs. For example, investigators have recently detected lupus autoantibodies in serum that often are present years before the patient displays symptoms. In another study on rheumatoid arthritis, high concentrations of autoantibodies and T cells in the blood were found to be predictive of rapid disease progression.

The Components of the Immune System

National Institute of Allergy and Infectious Diseases

In the following viewpoint the National Institute of Allergy and Infectious Diseases (NIAID) describes the components that make up the complex human immune system. According to the NIAID, the key to a properly functioning immune system is the ability to distinguish between the body's own cells and those of foreign invaders, such as microorganisms. When this ability is compromised, autoimmune diseases and allergies are the result. The NIAID describes the major components of the immune system, including the different immune cells and what they do, the organs that produce the immune cells, and one of the communication cells of the immune system. The NIAID is one of the twenty-seven institutes and centers that make up the National Institutes of Health. The NIAID promotes research that leads to understanding, treatment, and ultimately prevention of the myriad of infectious, immunologic, and allergic diseases that threaten millions of human lives.

The immune system is a network of cells, tissues, and organs that work together to defend the body against attacks by "foreign" invaders. These are primarily microbes—tiny organisms such as bacteria,

SOURCE: Courtesy National Institute of Allergy and Infectious Diseases.

parasites, and fungi that can cause infections. Viruses also cause infections, but are too primitive to be classified as living organisms. The human body provides an ideal environment for many microbes. It is the immune system's job to keep them out or, failing that, to seek out and destroy them.

When the immune system hits the wrong target, however, it can unleash a torrent of disorders, including allergic diseases, arthritis, and a form of diabetes. If the immune system is crippled, other kinds of diseases result.

A Complex System

The immune system is amazingly complex. It can recognize and remember millions of different enemies, and it can produce secretions (release of fluids) and cells to match up with and wipe out nearly all of them.

The secret to its success is an elaborate and dynamic communications network. Millions and millions of cells, organized into sets and subsets, gather like clouds of bees swarming around a hive and pass information back and forth in response to an infection. Once immune cells receive the alarm, they become activated and begin to produce powerful chemicals. These substances allow the cells to regulate their own growth and behavior, enlist other immune cells, and direct the new recruits to trouble spots.

Although scientists have learned much about the immune system, they continue to study how the body launches attacks that destroy invading microbes, infected cells, and tumors while ignoring healthy tissues. New technologies for identifying individual immune cells are now allowing scientists to determine quickly which targets are triggering an immune response. Improvements in microscopy are permitting the first-ever observations of living B cells, T cells, and other cells as they interact within lymph nodes and other body tissues.

In addition, scientists are rapidly unraveling the genetic blueprints that direct the human immune response, as well as those that dictate the biology of bacteria, viruses, and parasites. The combination of new technology and expanded genetic information will no doubt reveal even more about how the body protects itself from disease. . . .

The key to a healthy immune system is its remarkable ability to distinguish between the body's own cells, recognized as "self," and foreign cells, or "nonself." The body's immune defenses normally coexist peacefully with cells that carry distinctive "self" marker molecules. But when immune defenders encounter foreign cells or organisms carrying markers that say "nonself," they quickly launch an attack.

Anything that can trigger this immune response is called an antigen. An antigen can be a microbe such as a virus, or a part of a microbe such as a molecule. Tissues or cells from another person (except an identical twin) also carry nonself markers and act as foreign antigens. This explains why tissue transplants may be rejected.

In abnormal situations, the immune system can mistake self for nonself and launch an attack against the body's own cells or tissues. The result is called an autoimmune disease. Some forms of arthritis and diabetes are autoimmune diseases.

In other cases, the immune system responds to a seemingly harmless foreign substance such as ragweed pollen. The result is allergy, and this kind of antigen is called an allergen. . . .

Immune System Organs

The organs of the immune system are positioned throughout the body. They are called lymphoid organs because they are home to lymphocytes, small white blood cells that are the key players in the immune system.

Organs of the Immune System

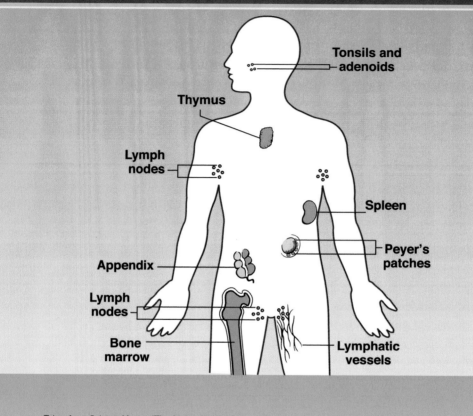

Taken from: Science Master, "The Anatomy of the Immune System," www.sciencemaster.com/jump/life/immune.php.

Bone marrow, the soft tissue in the hollow center of bones, is the ultimate source of all blood cells, including lymphocytes. The thymus is a lymphoid organ that lies behind the breastbone.

Lymphocytes known as T lymphocytes or T cells ("T" stands for "thymus") mature in the thymus and then migrate to other tissues. B lymphocytes, also known as B cells, become activated and mature into plasma cells, which make and release antibodies.

Lymph nodes, which are located in many parts of the body, are lymphoid tissues that contain numerous specialized structures.

T cells from the thymus concentrate in the paracortex [of the lymph node]. B cells develop in and around the germinal centers. Plasma cells occur in the medulla.

Lymphocytes can travel throughout the body using the blood vessels. The cells can also travel through a system of lymphatic vessels that closely parallels the body's veins and arteries.

Cells and fluids are exchanged between blood and lymphatic vessels, enabling the lymphatic system to monitor the body for invading microbes. The lymphatic vessels carry lymph, a clear fluid that bathes the body's tissues.

Small, bean-shaped lymph nodes are laced along the lymphatic vessels, with clusters in the neck, armpits, abdomen, and groin. Each lymph node contains specialized compartments where immune cells congregate, and where they can encounter antigens.

Immune cells, microbes, and foreign antigens enter the lymph nodes via incoming lymphatic vessels or the lymph nodes' tiny blood vessels. All lymphocytes exit lymph nodes through outgoing lymphatic vessels. Once in the bloodstream, lymphocytes are transported to tissues throughout the body. They patrol everywhere for foreign antigens, then gradually drift back into the lymphatic system to begin the cycle all over again.

The spleen is a flattened organ at the upper left of the abdomen. Like the lymph nodes, the spleen contains specialized compartments where immune cells gather and work. The spleen serves as a meeting ground where immune defenses confront antigens.

Other clumps of lymphoid tissue are found in many parts of the body, especially in the linings of the digestive tract, airways, and lungs—territories that serve as gateways to the body. These tissues include the tonsils, adenoids, and appendix. . . .

Immune Cells

The immune system stockpiles a huge arsenal of cells, not only lymphocytes but also cell-devouring phagocytes and their relatives. Some immune cells take on all intruders, whereas others are trained on highly specific targets. To work effectively, most immune cells need the cooperation of their comrades. Sometimes immune cells communicate by direct physical contact, and sometimes they communicate releasing chemical messengers.

The immune system stores just a few of each kind of the different cells needed to recognize millions of possible enemies. When an antigen first appears, the few immune cells that can respond to it multiply into a full-scale army of cells. After their job is done, the immune cells fade away, leaving sentries behind to watch for future attacks.

All immune cells begin as immature stem cells in the bone marrow. They respond to different cytokines and other chemical signals to grow into specific immune cell types, such as T cells, B cells, or phagocytes. Because stem cells have not yet committed to a particular future, their use presents an interesting possibility for treating some immune system disorders. Researchers currently are investigating if a person's own stem cells can be used to regenerate damaged immune responses in autoimmune diseases and in immune deficiency disorders, such as HIV infection. . . .

B Cells and T Cells

B cells and T cells are the main types of lymphocytes. B cells work chiefly by secreting substances called antibodies into the body's fluids. Antibodies ambush foreign antigens circulating in the bloodstream. They are powerless, however, to penetrate cells. The job of attacking target cells—either cells that have been infected by viruses or cells that have been distorted by cancer—is left to T cells or other immune cells.

Each B cell is programmed to make one specific antibody. For example, one B cell will make an antibody that blocks a virus that causes the common cold, while another produces an antibody that attacks a bacterium that causes pneumonia. When a B cell encounters the kind of antigen that triggers it to become active, it gives rise to many large cells known as plasma cells, which produce antibodies.

Immunoglobulin G, or IgG, is a kind of antibody that works efficiently to coat microbes, speeding their uptake by other cells in the immune system. IgM is very effective at killing bacteria. IgA concentrates in body fluids—tears, saliva, and the secretions of the respiratory and digestive tracks—guarding the entrances to the body. IgE, whose natural job probably is to protect against parasitic infections, is responsible for the symptoms of allergy. IgD remains attached to B cells and plays a key role in initiating early B cell responses.

Unlike B cells, T cells do not recognize free-floating antigens. Rather, their surfaces contain specialized antibody-like receptors that see fragments of antigens on the surfaces of infected or cancerous cells. T cells contribute to immune defenses in two major ways: Some direct and regulate immune responses, whereas others directly attack infected or cancerous cells.

Helper T cells, or Th cells, coordinate immune responses by communicating with other cells. Some stimulate nearby B cells to produce antibodies, others call in microbe-gobbling cells called phagocytes, and still others activate other T cells.

Cytotoxic T lymphocytes (CTLs)—also called killer T cells—perform a different function. These cells directly attack other cells carrying certain foreign or abnormal molecules on their surfaces. CTLs are especially useful for attacking viruses because viruses often hide from other parts of the immune system while they grow inside infected cells. CTLs recognize small fragments of these viruses peeking out from the cell membrane and launch an attack to kill the infected cell.

FAST FACT

According to *The Molecular Biology of the Cell,* immune cells constitute about 1 percent of the volume of blood in a human.

In most cases, T cells only recognize an antigen if it is carried on the surface of a cell by one of the body's own major histocompatibility complex, or MHC, molecules. MHC molecules are proteins recognized by T cells when they distinguish between self and nonself. A self-MHC molecule provides a recognizable scaffolding to present a foreign antigen to the T cell. In humans, MHC antigens are called human leukocyte antigens, or HLA.

Although MHC molecules are required for T cell responses against foreign invaders, they also create problems during organ transplantations. Virtually every cell in the

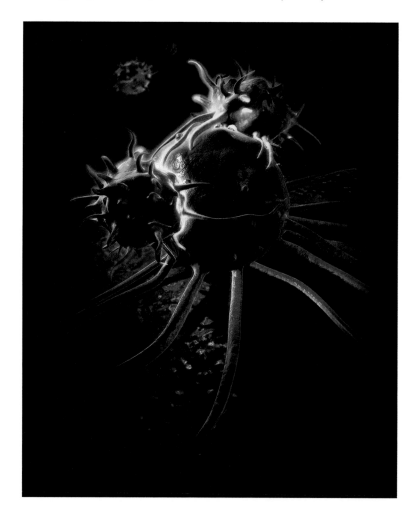

This illustration shows two cytotoxic T cells attacking a single cancer cell. T cells originate in the thymus, come in a variety of types, and play a role in the immune system. **(Marc Phares/Photo Researchers, Inc.)**

body is covered with MHC proteins, but each person has a different set of these proteins on his or her cells. If a T cell recognizes a nonself-MHC molecule on another cell, it will destroy the cell. Therefore, doctors must match organ recipients with donors who have the closest MHC make-up. Otherwise the recipient's T cells will likely attack the transplanted organ, leading to graft rejection.

Natural killer (NK) cells are another kind of lethal white cell, or lymphocyte. Like CTLs, NK cells are armed with granules filled with potent chemicals. But CTLs look for antigen fragments bound to self-MHC molecules, whereas NK cells recognize cells lacking self-MHC molecules. Thus, NK cells have the potential to attack many types of foreign cells.

Both kinds of killer cells slay on contact. The deadly assassins bind to their targets, aim their weapons, and then deliver a lethal burst of chemicals.

T cells aid the normal processes of the immune system. If NK T cells fail to function properly, asthma, certain autoimmune diseases—including Type 1 diabetes—or the growth of cancers may result. NK T cells get their name because they are a kind of T lymphocyte that carries some of the surface proteins, called "markers," typical of NK T cells. But these T cells differ from other kinds of T cells. They do not recognize pieces of antigen bound to self-MHC molecules. Instead, they recognize fatty substances (lipids and glycolipids) that are bound to a different class of molecules called CD1d. Scientists are trying to discover methods to control the timing and release of chemical factors by NK T cells, with the hope they can modify immune responses in ways that benefit patients. . . .

Phagocytes and Their Relatives

Phagocytes are large white cells that can swallow and digest microbes and other foreign particles. Monocytes are phagocytes that circulate in the blood. When monocytes migrate into tissues, they develop into macrophages.

Specialized types of macrophages can be found in many organs, including the lungs, kidneys, brain, and liver.

Macrophages play many roles. As scavengers, they rid the body of worn-out cells and other debris. They display bits of foreign antigen in a way that draws the attention of matching lymphocytes . . . and they churn out an amazing variety of powerful chemical signals, known as monokines, which are vital to the immune response.

Granulocytes are another kind of immune cell. They contain granules filled with potent chemicals, which allow the granulocytes to destroy microorganisms. Some of these chemicals, such as histamine, also contribute to inflammation and allergy.

One type of granulocyte, the neutrophil, is also a phagocyte. Neutrophils use their prepackaged chemicals to break down the microbes they ingest. Eosinophils and basophils are granulocytes that "degranulate" by spraying their chemicals onto harmful cells or microbes nearby.

Mast cells function much like basophils, except they are not blood cells. Rather, they are found in the lungs, skin, tongue, and linings of the nose and intestinal tract, where they contribute to the symptoms of allergy.

Related structures, called blood platelets, are cell fragments. Platelets also contain granules. In addition to promoting blood clotting and wound repair, platelets activate some immune defenses.

Dendritic cells are found in the parts of lymphoid organs where T cells also exist. Like macrophages, dendritic cells in lymphoid tissues display antigens to T cells and help stimulate T cells during an immune response. They are called dendritic cells because they have branchlike extensions that can interlace to form a network. . . .

Cytokines: Messengers of the Immune System

Cells of the immune system communicate with one another by releasing and responding to chemical messengers called cytokines. These proteins are secreted by immune cells and act on other cells to coordinate appropriate immune responses. Cytokines include a diverse assortment of interleukins, interferons, and growth factors.

Some cytokines are chemical switches that turn certain immune cell types on and off. One cytokine, interleukin 2 (IL-2), triggers the immune system to produce T cells. IL-2's immunity-boosting properties have traditionally made it a promising treatment for several illnesses. Clinical studies are underway to test its benefits in diseases such as cancer, hepatitis C, and HIV infection and AIDS. Scientists are studying other cytokines to see whether they can also be used to treat diseases.

One group of cytokines chemically attracts specific cell types. These so-called chemokines are released by cells at a site of injury or infection and call other immune cells to the region to help repair the damage or fight off the invader. Chemokines often play a key role in inflammation and are a promising target for new drugs to help regulate immune responses.

What Autoimmune Diseases Have in Common

Noel R. Rose

In the following viewpoint Noel R. Rose discusses the common causes of autoimmune diseases. According to Rose, autoimmunity and autoimmune disease are distinct concepts. Autoimmunity arises when the immune system attacks the self, while autoimmune disease is a disorder *caused* by autoimmunity. Rose says autoimmunity is the common thread that links all the different autoimmune diseases together. However, autoimmunity alone is not sufficient to cause an autoimmune disease. Rose asserts that a person's genetic makeup and certain triggers in the environment also come into play. He hopes that research into the common causes of autoimmune diseases will someday lead to a cure. Rose is the chair emeritus of the American Autoimmune Related Diseases Association National Scientific Advisory Board, a professor of molecular microbiology and immunology, and the director of the Center for Autoimmune Disease Research at the Bloomberg School of Public Health at Johns Hopkins University.

SOURCE: Noel R. Rose, "The Common Thread," American Autoimmune Related Diseases Association, Inc., 2004–2010. Reproduced by permission.

What happened about 40 years ago? Well, a number of key discoveries were made—some of them in my own laboratory—which turned that doctrine of self, non-self distinction [where the immune system will distinguish between the host body and a foreign invader] on its head. We found that there are a number of instances in which the immune response is directed to something in the body of the host itself. It seemed implausible, even contradictory; but, in fact, that was exactly what we found: there are some circumstances where the immune response attacks the body of the host itself. The host may be an animal or it may be a human patient. That is what we call autoimmunity. Autoimmunity is nothing more than the immune response directed to the body of the patient himself or herself.

Autoimmunity and Autoimmune Disease

Let me define a second term for you, autoimmune disease. These two terms do not mean exactly the same thing, and the difference may be important to us as we talk about some of these issues. . . . Autoimmune disease is a disorder that occurs because of autoimmunity—a disease that is caused by an immune response to the body of the patient himself or herself.

Now, in defining autoimmune disease that way, I imply that there is autoimmunity without autoimmune disease. In fact, we now know that autoimmunity is not at all uncommon and that it exists in all of us. Every one of us has some degree of autoimmunity naturally, and it does not seem to do us any harm. It is, in fact, only a minority of cases where autoimmunity actually produces damage in the body, producing disease. So there are really two basic questions that I, as an investigator, and my colleagues in this field [immunology] need to unravel.

First question is: How does autoimmunity arise? What causes the body to produce an immune response to itself? What are the circumstances, what are the mechanisms, what are the triggers for the phenomenon that we call autoimmunity? That's one question. That's a very basic question that involves biology, chemistry, even biophysics. It requires a deep understanding of the immune system. We need to know a lot more about how the body produces immunity reactions. We know a great deal, but there are still enormous voids in our understanding. We must know that in order to understand how the body normally distinguishes self from non-self.

The second question is: What are the factors in the autoimmune response that sometimes cause disease? These are the two critical questions that are the topics of basic research. Sometimes the feeling is expressed that basic research is scientists fooling around in the laboratory doing things that are unimportant. Well, there is nothing that is unimportant about these questions. They are absolutely critical. We must understand that if we are ever going to develop effective treatments or, more important, cures for preventing autoimmune disease, we must understand them. Just as we would never have been able to control infectious diseases until we found the bacteria or viruses that cause diseases, so we cannot deal effectively with autoimmune disease until we understand its cause. . . .

Why are autoimmune diseases related? . . . Here I have to give you a little bit of insider information about how medicine is organized in this country. . . .

The Etiology of Disease

When medicine grew up in the middle ages, physicians had to divide diseases into various kinds and various categories. The only way they could classify diseases was anatomically, that is, where does the disease occur? Physicians later divided themselves into doctors who were interested in diseases of the lungs, and other doctors who were interested in diseases of the skin, and other doctors were interested in disease of the intestinal tract or the reproductive tract or the urinary tract. Most medicine is still organized on the basis of the anatomy of the disease, on where the disease occurs. You go to a heart specialist (a cardiologist) if you have heart disease, to a neurologist if you have nervous system disease, to a dermatologist if you have a skin disease, and on and on. The medical community organized itself that way because that's all the doctors knew. They didn't know what caused disease, but they knew where it occurred. But starting with Louis Pasteur about a hundred years ago, a change occurred. For the very first time we began to understand why disease occurs—not where it occurs, but why it occurs. And when we speak of why disease occurs, we speak of something else, and that is what we call etiology.

Etiology means cause, why the disease occurs. If we are concerned with curing disease and possibly even preventing disease, the etiology is the most important information. Why have we been able to control so many infectious diseases? Because we now know the bacteria and the viruses and the parasites that cause these diseases, and we can develop antibiotics and other drugs that will specifically attack that organism. Discovering the etiology has allowed medicine to progress to its present state where we can successfully treat and even cure many diseases.

Within the lifetime of most of us, we have ways of effectively treating infectious disease. Until World War II, until antibiotics were introduced, we did not have methods that cured disease. We had treatments that alleviated the symptoms of disease, but we really didn't cure disease. With the introduction of antibiotics—penicillin, streptomycin, and other substances—we now have a way of treating. And that's why it is so important to understand etiology.

Here are a few other groups of diseases which are now defined by their etiology. Allergies are an example. If you

> **FAST FACT**
>
> According to the American Autoimmune Related Diseases Association, autoimmunity is the underlying cause of more than one hundred serious, chronic illnesses.

have an allergy, it doesn't matter whether it's an allergy of the nose, that is, hay fever, whether it's in the lungs, asthma, or whether it's atopic dermatitis, a skin disease. You may go to an allergist because all of these diseases have the same etiology. They have different anatomies, but they have the same etiology. That's the way progress is being made by bringing together diseases with the same etiology.

Autoimmunity as an Etiology

Autoimmunity is an etiology: It is a cause of disease. Anatomically, autoimmune disease is very diverse; and that's why we see specialists in so many areas of medicine studying autoimmunity. They may be rheumatologists who are interested in joints; they may be dermatologists who are interested in skin; they may be cardiologists who are interested in the heart; they may be gastroenterologists who are interested in the gastrointestinal tract. But the common etiology for all of these disease—for Crohn's disease of the gut; for lupus of the skin; for rheumatoid arthritis of the joint—the common etiology that brings together all of these diseases is autoimmunity.

A major aim of the American Autoimmune Related Diseases Association is to help us to understand that all of these diseases, diverse as they are, in their anatomical location, in their clinical manifestation, are related because they have the same etiology; they are all caused by autoimmunity. In my opinion, the only way we're going to develop really effective treatments will be to treat the cause of the disease, not the symptoms. The symptoms are late; the symptoms are at the end of the train of events. We want to get on the train at the very beginning.

Now, what are some of the specifics of this relationship? Let me lay out some of the principles that we now understand about the etiology of autoimmune disease.

Unlike some diseases, autoimmune diseases do not generally have a simple, single cause. There are usually two major categories of factors that are involved in causing autoimmune diseases: genetics and environment. Virtually every autoimmune disease combines these two. Let me explain more of what I mean. First, genetics. Genetics is involved in the development of autoimmune disease, but autoimmune diseases are not typical genetic diseases. What is a typical genetic disease? Most of us have heard of sickle cell anemia, and that's a genetic disease. That's a disease in which the victims of the disease have a specific genetic mutation. If you inherit this mutation from one parent, you have sickle cell trait; and if you inherit it from both parents, you have sickle cell disease. We know what the gene is, and we even know a great deal of how that works; so we know the etiology of that disease. . . .

Lesions produced by lupus are shown here. Lupus, rheumatoid arthritis, and Crohn's disease all have a common etiology, or cause: autoimmunity. **(Biophoto Associates/ Photo Researchers, Inc.)**

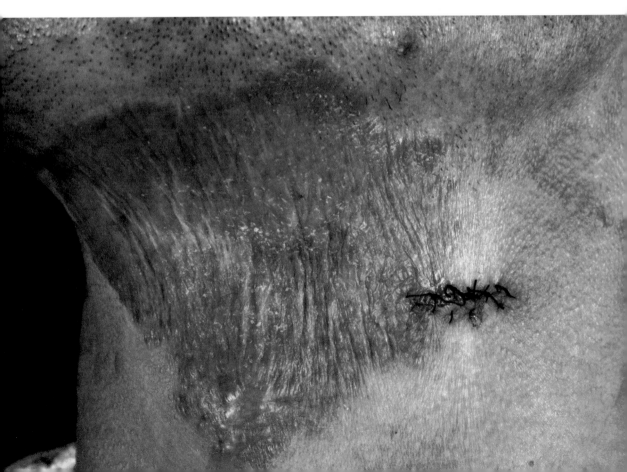

The Genetic Basis of Autoimmune Disease

That's not the way genetics works in autoimmune disease. In autoimmune disease, multiple genes are involved; we have genes that collectively increase the vulnerability or susceptibility to autoimmune disease. What is inherited is not a specific gene that causes a specific defect in metabolism; several genes increase vulnerability or susceptibility to autoimmune disease.

How do we know that there is a genetic basis of autoimmune disease? I can cite three kinds of evidence. The first is autoimmune diseases tend to occur in families. If there's one case of autoimmune disease in the family, there's likely to be another case.

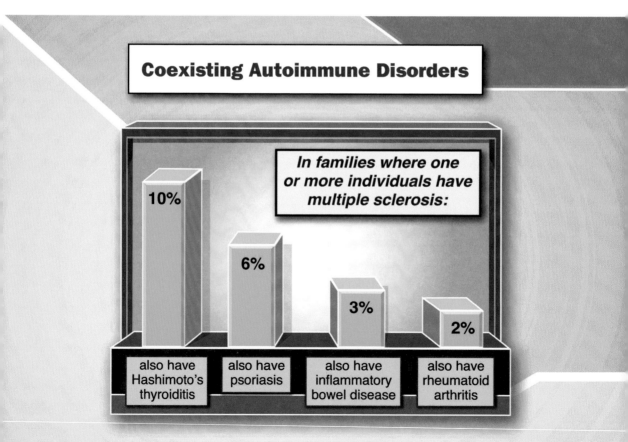

Coexisting Autoimmune Disorders

In families where one or more individuals have multiple sclerosis:

10% also have Hashimoto's thyroiditis

6% also have psoriasis

3% also have inflammatory bowel disease

2% also have rheumatoid arthritis

Taken from: L.F. Barcellos et al. "Clustering of Autoimmune Diseases in Families with a High Risk for Multiple Sclerosis: A Descriptive Study," *Lancet Neurology*, November 5, 2006.

However, it is not a particular autoimmune disease; it is generally a tendency to autoimmunity. One family member may have lupus, another family member may have Sjögren's disease, a third member of the family may have rheumatoid arthritis. That's one bit of evidence for genetic involvement, and we've known this for a number of years. If we ask patients when they come to us, "Is there other autoimmune disease in your family?"—and we actually have to mention them because people don't know these are all autoimmune diseases—they will usually say, "Yes, my aunt had thyroid trouble . . . my grandmother had that disease . . . my grandmother had Crohn's disease. . . ."

But we call this soft data in science because families share genes and that's some indication of genetics; but families share other things.

So we need to look further. The second thing we do is to look at twins. We compare two kinds of twins. There are twins that are genetically identical, and there are twins that are non-genetically identical. If something is caused by an environmental factor, there should be no difference between identical twins and non-identical twins. If there's a difference, it suggests that genetics plays a role. These studies have been done for a number of autoimmune diseases, and the answer has always come up about the same. Genetic components represent something in the order of half of the risks. In other words, if you have a genetic predisposition to autoimmunity, you may have twice or five times as much chance of developing autoimmunity as someone else—not 100 times, but not zero. So genetics plays an important role.

One group of genetic factors is particularly important. One of the things that immunology has taught us through the years is obvious but needed some kind of physical basis, it is simply that every human being is different from every other human being (unless you have a genetically identical twin). Every person is a little different from everybody else; we know that for certain when we try to transplant tissues, like kidneys or hearts. In general you cannot accept a kidney or heart from someone else unless we dampen your immune response.

There clearly are significant physical differences between different people. And we call the substance that causes that difference histocompatibility complex. We call the genes that provide that difference "major histocompatibility complex genes." Everybody abbreviates that long tongue twister by just saying MHC; and every species has an MHC, a major histocompatibility gene. In a human we call it HLA [human leukocyte antigen].

HLA is the major group of genes that distinguishes one human being from another. It is important in transplantation, and we do HLA typing regularly. It's important to us in autoimmunity because susceptibility to autoimmunity is associated with the HLA type. It represents the most important single genetic trait in estimating susceptibility to autoimmune disease.

There are three kinds of information that tell us if autoimmune diseases are genetic. I've mentioned two. One is family clustering; the second is the association with HLA. What's the third?

The third is that autoimmune diseases occur in animals as well as in human beings. With animals we can do the breedings that are necessary.

We can infer the same must be true in humans. In animals the equivalent of HLA determines susceptibility. In animals this trait is actually predictive. In humans we aren't yet at that point because we don't have enough information from humans to say, "Because of your HLA factor you're going to develop an autoimmune disease." We can, however, say that you have a greater likelihood of this happening.

So we're getting to a point where we can almost predict who is more likely or less likely to develop autoimmune disease. Now this, again, is an example of how very basic research on a molecular level or on a genetic molecular level is beginning to pay off in human medicine.

The Other Risk Factor: Environment

I would like to conclude with the second half of the story. I've said that genetics accounts for about half of the risk that you develop an autoimmune disease.

The other half is the agent in the environment which triggers the process. Unfortunately, we do not know very many of the triggers. We know there are certain drugs that can induce lupus. We know there are certain environmental substances like silica that can induce scleroderma. We suspect that there are certain dietary substances, such as iodine, that can exacerbate thyroid disease. So we're beginning to define the other half of the story, the environmental half. It is going to be, I think, an equally fascinating chapter in the saga of autoimmune disease in the next decade.

So, in summary, that's what autoimmune diseases have in common. That's why we feel very strongly there should be a society like the American Autoimmune Related Diseases Association that brings together all of the research and all of the investigators and all of the physicians as well as all of the patients interested in autoimmune diseases. Let us begin to get to questions of etiology, to get at the root causes of these diseases, rather than being left at the superficial level, that is, treating the symptoms after the disease has had its destructive effects.

Genes Play a Key Role in Autoimmune Diseases

David Cameron

In the following viewpoint David Cameron discusses the discovery of a key set of genes that could lead to new therapies for autoimmune diseases. According to Cameron, researchers at the Massachusetts Institute of Technology, the Whitehead Institute, and the Dana-Farber Cancer Institute have identified a set of genes that constitute a key part of the autoimmune response. The genes, says Cameron, link the body's master immune response regulator—a gene called Foxp3—to the body's regulatory T cells. It is the regulatory T cells' job to prevent immune cells from attacking the body's own tissues and organs. The discovery is helping scientists to understand what causes regulatory T cells to stop doing their job. Cameron is senior science writer at the Whitehead Institute for Biomedical Research.

Autoimmune diseases such as type 1 diabetes, lupus and rheumatoid arthritis occur when the immune system fails to regulate itself. But researchers have not known precisely where the molecular breakdowns responsible for such failures occur.

SOURCE: David Cameron, "Discovery Could Lead to New Therapies for Diabetes, Lupus and Arthritis," *MIT Tech Talk,* vol. 51, January 24, 2007, pp. 5–6. Reproduced by permission.

Now, scientists from MIT [Massachusetts Institute of Technology], the Whitehead Institute and the Dana-Farber Cancer Institute have identified a key set of genes that lie at the core of autoimmune disease, findings that may help scientists develop new methods for manipulating immune system activity.

"This may shorten the path to new therapies for autoimmune disease," said Whitehead member and MIT professor of biology Richard Young, senior author on a paper that appeared online in *Nature* on Jan. 21 [2007]. "With this new list of genes, we can now look for possible therapies with far greater precision."

The Master Regulator of the Frontline Immune Response

The immune system is often described as a kind of military unit, a defense network that guards the body from invaders. Seen in this way, a group of white blood cells called T cells are the frontline soldiers of immune defense, engaging invading pathogens head-on.

These T cells are commanded by a second group of cells called regulatory T cells. Regulatory T cells prevent biological "friendly fire" by ensuring that the T cells do not attack the body's own tissues. Failure of the regulatory T cells to control the frontline fighters leads to autoimmune disease.

Scientists previously discovered that regulatory T cells are themselves controlled by a master gene regulator called Foxp3. Master gene regulators bind to specific genes and control their level of activity, which in turn affects the behavior of cells.

In fact, when Foxp3 stops functioning, the body can no longer produce working regulatory T cells. When this happens, the frontline T cells damage multiple organs and cause symptoms of type 1 diabetes and Crohn's

> **FAST FACT**
>
> According to the American Autoimmune Related Diseases Association, a close genetic relationship exists among autoimmune diseases, explaining clustering in individuals and families as well as a common pathway of disease.

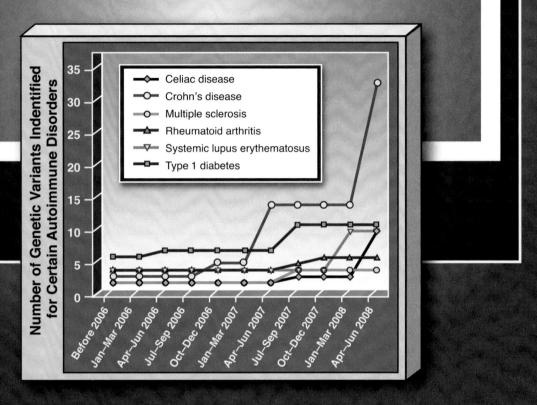

Rise in Discovery of Genetic Risk Factors for Autoimmune Disorders

Taken from: Guillaume Lettre and John Rioux, "Autoimmune Diseases: Insights from Genome-Wide Association Studies," *Human Molecular Genetics*, 2008.

disease. However, until now, scientists have barely understood how Foxp3 controls regulatory T cells because they knew almost nothing about the actual genes under Foxp3's purview.

Locating the Genes Controlled by the Master Regulator

Researchers in Young's lab, working closely with immunologist Harald von Boehmer of the Dana-Farber Cancer Institute, used a DNA microarray technology developed by Young to scan the entire genome of T cells and locate

PERSPECTIVES ON DISEASES AND DISORDERS

the genes controlled by Foxp3. There were roughly 30 genes found to be directly controlled by Foxp3 and one, called Ptpn22, showed a particularly strong affinity.

"This relation was striking because Ptpn22 is strongly associated with type 1 diabetes, rheumatoid arthritis, lupus and Graves' disease, but the gene had not been previously linked to regulatory T-cell function," said Alexander Marson, an M.D.-Ph.D. student in the Young lab and lead author on the paper. "Discovering this correlation was a big moment for us. It verified that we were on the right track for identifying autoimmune-related genes."

The researchers still don't know exactly how Foxp3 enables regulatory T cells to prevent autoimmunity. But the list of the genes that Foxp3 targets provides an initial map of the circuitry of these cells, which is important for understanding how they control a healthy immune response.

Researchers are now using DNA microarray technology to monitor the interactions of thousands of genes simultaneously on a single chip. (**Sam Ogden/PhotoResearchers, Inc.**)

"Autoimmune diseases take a tremendous toll on human health, but on a strictly molecular level, autoimmunity is a black box," said Young. "When we discover the molecular mechanisms that drive these conditions, we can migrate from treating symptoms to developing treatments for the disease itself."

Autoimmune Diseases Affect More Women than Men

Andrew Pollack

In the following viewpoint Andrew Pollack discusses the gender disparity present in autoimmune diseases. According to Pollack, women outnumber men, in some cases by an 8 to 1 ratio, in having an autoimmune disease. The reasons for the gender disparity are not fully known, although scientists theorize that female hormones play a key role in causing the diseases. Pollack discusses the challenges faced by women when they become stricken with one or more of the many different autoimmune diseases. Pollack covers biotechnology issues for the *New York Times*.

R oxanne Perez had never really been sick in her life until, at age 27, the roof began falling in. During a Fourth of July weekend at the beach in 2000, she was rushed to an emergency room suffering from convulsions. In the months after, she had blood transfusions and her spleen removed. Then, in 2001, she suffered a heart attack that left her heart permanently weakened.

SOURCE: Andrew Pollack, "Trying to Shut Off the Body's Friendly Fire," *New York Times,* June 5, 2005. Reproduced by permission.

Ms. Perez, who lives in San Antonio [Texas], had to give up her job, her home and car and move in with her parents. Now 32, she suffers from frequent fatigue, made worse when she goes out in the sun, and takes 25 different drugs. She said she could never have children.

"I was at the prime of my life and it's like a bomb fell on me," she said.

The attack was the physiological equivalent of friendly fire. Ms. Perez has lupus and hemolytic anemia. Both are autoimmune diseases, in which the person's immune system, meant to defend against germs, instead directs its fury against the person's own tissues.

There are at least 80 autoimmune diseases, ranging from familiar ones like rheumatoid arthritis, psoriasis, multiple sclerosis and Type 1 diabetes to more obscure ones like pemphigus vulgaris. They affect 5 to 8 percent of the American population, or up to 23.5 million people, say estimates from the National Institutes of Health [NIH]. Patient advocacy groups often give much higher estimates, and there is evidence that the incidence of some of the diseases is increasing.

Gender Disparity

Most of the victims are women—many, like Ms. Perez, in their childbearing years. There are at least eight women for every man who has lupus, scleroderma, thyroiditis and Sjögren's syndrome. Women also outnumber men, though not by as large a margin, for multiple sclerosis, rheumatoid arthritis and inflammatory bowel disease.

The reasons for the gender disparity are not known, though there are theories. In fact, little is definitively known about the causes of autoimmune diseases or how to treat them. It has been more than 30 years since a new drug was approved for lupus, for instance, and the existing drugs have severe side effects.

But scientists are now using genetics and biotechnology to gradually unravel the mind-boggling complexity of the immune system.

"It's a very vibrant field right now," said Dr. Noel R. Rose, the director of the Center for Autoimmune Disease Research at Johns Hopkins University and chairman of a committee to coordinate the $600 million in autoimmune disease research at the N.I.H.

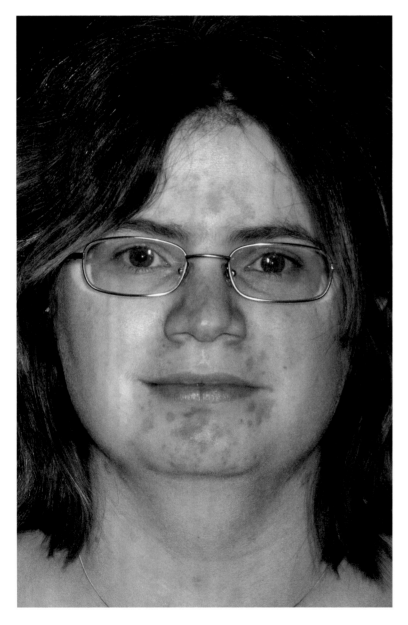

A woman suffers from the symptoms of the autoimmune disorder psoriasis, a reddish, scaly rash. Women with autoimmune diseases outnumber men by eight to one. (Dr. P. Marrazi/Photo Researchers, Inc.)

Even the formation of Dr. Rose's committee, required by an act of Congress in 2000, is a sign of progress. In the past, each disease was thought of separately, discouraging scientists from sharing findings that might apply to more than one disease. And since most of the diseases by themselves are rare, there was not much incentive for drug companies to develop treatments. That is changing.

"Just in the last five years, they are now considered a category like cancer is considered a disease category," said Virginia T. Ladd, president of the American Autoimmune Related Diseases Association, a patient advocacy group in Eastpointe, Mich. "Eventually we should have an autoimmunologist like we have an oncologist."

In autoimmune disease, something goes awry with the process in which the immune system learns to distinguish self from non-self, the body's own tissues from that of an invading germ.

The diseases can run in families and some people get more than one. "If you live long enough you get to collect them," said Ms. Ladd, who has lupus, antiphospholipid syndrome, pernicious anemia and vasculitis.

Scientists think that a combination of genes raises susceptibility. But evidence suggests that it takes an external factor to set off the disease. This could be something in the diet or a drug. But most attention is focused on infections by viruses or bacteria.

Rheumatic fever, for example, is a heart ailment incited by the bacterium that causes strep throat. In a small percentage of people, the immune system attacks a protein in the heart that closely resembles part of the bacterium.

As for the gender discrepancy, many scientists theorize that it results from women's hormones, like estrogen. This is partly because many of the ailments begin after puberty and tend to ease after menopause.

> **FAST FACT**
>
> Autoimmune diseases affect approximately 8 percent of the population, and 78 percent of those afflicted are women, according to a study published in the Centers for Disease Control and Prevention's *Emerging Infectious Diseases* journal.

Another theory is that immune attacks are set off by the presence of cells from another person in the bloodstream; women retain some cells from fetuses after pregnancy.

Dr. John Harley of the University of Oklahoma Health Sciences Center and the Oklahoma Medical Research Foundation said he believed that women having two X chromosomes and men only one plays a role. Men who have an extra X chromosome, a rare condition called Klinefelter's syndrome, have a higher rate of lupus than other men, Dr. Harley reported at a conference.

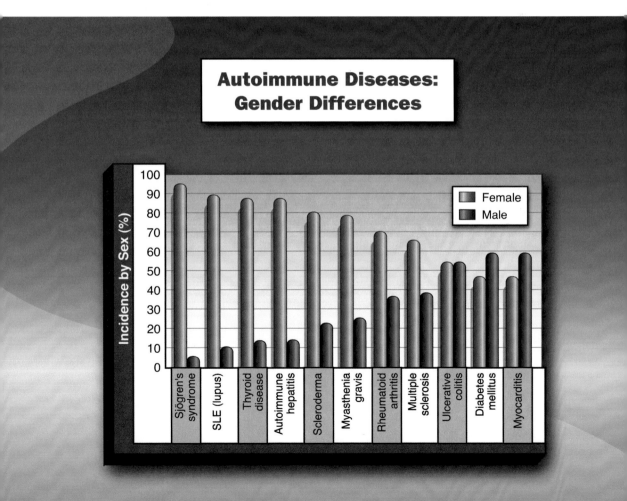

Taken from: DeLisa Fairweather and Noel Rose, "Women and Autoimmune Diseases," *Emerging Infectious Diseases*, Centers for Disease Control and Prevention, November 2004.

Difficult Diagnosis

Diagnosing autoimmune diseases can be difficult. Some women say it takes years of shuttling from doctor to doctor, often hearing that it is all in their heads.

"Every doctor has a specialty, and they only look through that one window," said Kerry Landhauser of West Islip, N.Y., who said it took six years for her Sjögren's syndrome to be diagnosed after she began experiencing bad headaches in 1997.

In Sjögren's, the immune system attacks moisture-producing glands like those that make saliva. At first, Mrs. Landhauser said, her dry mouth, a telltale symptom, was mistaken as a side effect of pills she was taking for her headaches.

Many autoimmune diseases are treated by suppressing the immune system with steroids or chemotherapy. But immune suppression leaves a person vulnerable to infections. It's "rather like taking a sledgehammer to the computer to try to slow it down," Dr. Harley said.

Newer treatments, many being developed by biotechnology companies, try to interfere with one part of the immune system rather than suppress it overall.

The biggest successes have been drugs that block tumor necrosis factor, a protein in the body that spurs inflammation. The three drugs in this class, Enbrel, Remicade and Humira, have had a major impact in slowing the joint damage caused by rheumatoid arthritis, and one or more of the drugs is also approved to treat psoriasis, Crohn's disease and ankylosing spondylitis.

But while the new biotech drugs seem to be better than steroids—and more expensive, costing more than $10,000 a year—they still dampen the immune system enough to raise the risk of infections or certain cancers.

That danger was illustrated in the case of Tysabri, a biotech drug that was heralded as a breakthrough for multiple sclerosis, then taken off the market in February

[2005] after it was linked to a rare and often fatal viral brain infection.

An ideal treatment would stop only the immune-system attack responsible for the disease while leaving the rest of the system working normally. In the future, it may also be possible to replace damaged tissue using stem cells.

Scientists are also seeking ways to detect the diseases before symptoms appear, by finding telltale antibodies in the blood or through genetic markers. "We'd like to try to intervene before the train wreck," said Dr. Rose of Johns Hopkins and the N.I.H.

A Novel Treatment Strives to Keep Autoimmunity in Check

Medical News Today

In the following viewpoint *Medical News Today* reports on a promising new approach to treating autoimmune diseases. According to *Medical News Today*, researchers at the Weizmann Institute in Israel have developed a method that may make it possible to treat autoimmunity effectively. Their development, called the "bystander approach," uses genetically engineered regulatory T cells—these are the cells that normally keep autoimmunity in check but go awry in autoimmune diseases—to zero in on the site of an autoimmune attack. *Medical News Today* is an Internet-based magazine that reports on medical advances and discoveries.

I n autoimmune diseases, the immune system turns against the body's own tissues and organs, wreaking havoc and destruction for no apparent reason. Partly because the origins of these diseases are so obscure, no effective treatment exists, and the suffering they inflict is enormous. Now Weizmann Institute scientists have

SOURCE: *Medical News Today*, "New Approach to Treating Autoimmune Disease Developed by Weizmann Institute Scientists," June 3, 2008. Reproduced by permission Weizmann Institute of Science.

developed a method that in the future may make it possible to treat autoimmune diseases effectively without necessarily knowing their exact cause. Their approach is equivalent to sending a police force to suppress a riot without seeking out the individuals who instigated the unrest.

In healthy people, a small but crucial group of immune cells called regulatory T cells, or T-regs, keeps autoimmunity in check, but in people with inflammatory bowel disease (IBD), one of the most common autoimmune disorders, too few of these cells appear in the diseased intestine, and the ones that do fail to function properly. The new Weizmann Institute approach consists of delivering highly selective, genetically engineered functioning T-regs to the intestine. The study was conducted by Dr. Eran Elinav, a physician from Tel Aviv Sourasky

One of the most common autoimmune diseases is inflammatory bowel disease. This computer artwork shows the typical inflammation, ulceration, and thickening of the intestinal lining, in red. (**David Mack/Photo Researchers, Inc.**)

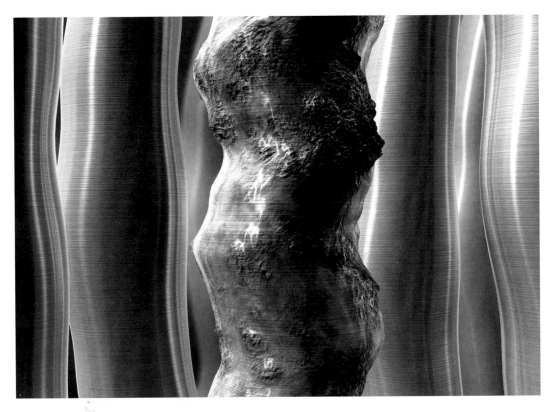

The Different Types of Regulatory T Cells

Regulatory T cells originate in the thymus. Naturally occurring regulatory T cells emerge from the thymus complete, while adaptive regulatory T cells are completed after they leave the thymus.

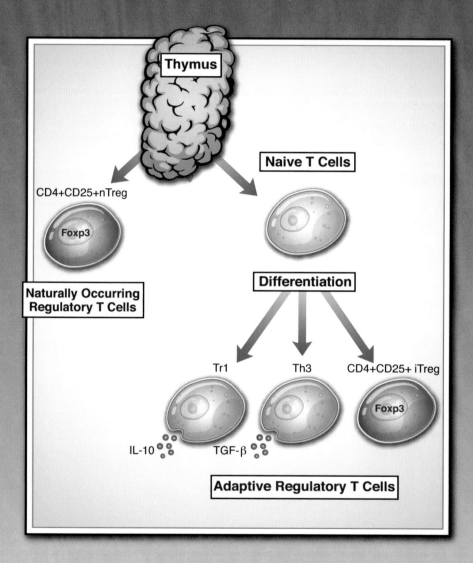

Thymus

CD4+CD25+nTreg

Foxp3

Naive T Cells

Naturally Occurring Regulatory T Cells

Differentiation

Tr1　Th3　CD4+CD25+ iTreg

Foxp3

IL-10　TGF-β

Adaptive Regulatory T Cells

Taken from: Dana Milojevic et al. "Regulatory T Cells and Their Role in Rheumatic Diseases: A Potential Target for Novel Therapeutic Development," *Pediatric Rheumatology*, December 2008.

Medical Center's gastroenterology institute who is working toward his Ph.D. at the Weizmann Institute, and lab assistant Tova Waks, in the laboratory of Prof. Zelig Eshhar of the Immunology Department.

The Bystander Approach

Relying on Eshhar's earlier work in which he equipped a different type of T cell to zero in on cancerous tumors, the team genetically engineered T-regs, outfitting these cells with a modular receptor consisting of three units. One of these units directed the cells to the intestine while the other two made sure they became duly activated. As reported in the journal *Gastroenterology*, the approach proved effective in laboratory mice with a disease that simulates human IBD: Most of the mice treated with the genetically-engineered T-regs developed only mild inflammation or no inflammation at all.

> **FAST FACT**
>
> Drugs to suppress the human immune response have been used since 1949, according to Medscape's eMedicine.

The cells produced what the scientists called a "bystander" effect: They were directed to the diseased tissue using neighboring, or "bystander" markers that identified the area as a site of inflammation, and suppressed the inflammatory cells in the vicinity by secreting soluble suppressive substances.

The scientists are currently [in June 2008] experimenting with human T-regs for curing ulcerative colitis and believe that in addition to IBD, their "bystander" approach could work in other autoimmune disorders, even if their causes remain unknown. They also think the method could be valuable in suppressing unwanted inflammation in diseases unrelated to autoimmunity, as well as in preventing graft rejection and certain complications in bone marrow and organ transplantation, in which inflammation is believed to play a major role.

A New Nanovaccine Could Treat Autoimmunity While Keeping the Immune System Intact

Cell

In the following viewpoint the journal *Cell* discusses the development of an autoimmune disease vaccine. According to *Cell*, researchers at the University of Calgary in Alberta, Canada, devised a vaccine made of nanoparticles. When administered to diabetic mice, the nano-based vaccine helped strengthen the mice's "good" T cells, enabling them to fight off the harmful T cells that were attacking insulin-producing cells and causing diabetes. *Cell* is a scientific journal that publishes research in various areas of life sciences.

A unique therapeutic nanovaccine that successfully reverses diabetes in a mouse model of the disease is providing new insight into diabetes, according to a study published in the online edition of the journal *Immunity*. It also reveals an aspect of the development of the autoimmune response that may provide a therapeutic strategy for multiple autoimmune disorders.

SOURCE: *Cell,* "'Nanovaccine' Reverses Autoimmunity Without General Immunosuppression," April 9, 2010. © 2010 Elsevier. Reproduced by permission.

Type 1 diabetes is a chronic autoimmune disease that results from destruction of insulin-producing pancreatic cells by certain white blood cells, called T cells. Eliminating the extensive repertoire of harmful T cells that attack the pancreas cannot currently be done without also eliminating T cells that protect us from infections and cancer, says Pere Santamaria, from the Julia McFarlane Diabetes Research Centre at the University of Calgary in Alberta.

Santamaria and colleagues wanted to find a way to counteract the harmful autoimmune response without compromising general immunity. They discovered that the body has a built-in mechanism that tries to stop the progression of autoimmune diseases like type 1 diabetes. They say there is an internal tug-of-war between aggressive T cells

FAST FACT

Cyclosporin, discovered in 1971, was the first immunosuppressive drug that acted selectively to suppress T cells, according to *Drug Discovery: A History*.

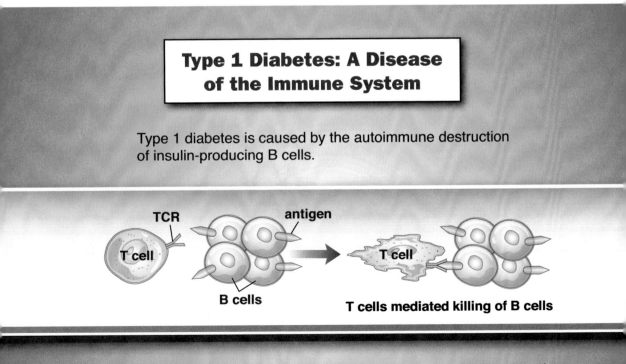

Type 1 Diabetes: A Disease of the Immune System

Type 1 diabetes is caused by the autoimmune destruction of insulin-producing B cells.

TCR

antigen

T cell

B cells

T cell

T cells mediated killing of B cells

Taken from: Mark Anderson, "Lecture: Autoimmunity," University of California Diabetes Center. http://immunology.ucsf.edu/immuno/courses/micro204/2009/Micro%20and%20imm20autoimmunity%20lecture%20final.pdf.

that want to cause the disease and weaker T cells that want to stop it from occurring.

Vaccine Made of Nanoparticles

The researchers developed a unique nanotechnology-based vaccine that selectively boosted the weak white blood T cells, enabling them to effectively counter the damage caused by their overactive T cell relatives. The vaccine consisted of nanoparticles coated with individual type 1 diabetes–relevant protein fragments bound to self MHC [major histocompatibility complex] molecules. MHC molecules are used by another type of white blood cell, called an "antigen-presenting cell" to "present" antigen to T cells as part of all immune responses.

Using a mouse model of type 1 diabetes, the researchers discovered that their nanovaccine blunted progression of the disease in prediabetic mice and restored normal

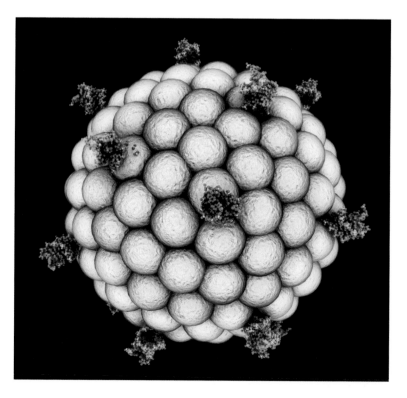

Computer artwork of a nanoparticle is shown here. Researchers are using nanoparticles coated with individual type 1 diabetes–relevant proteins to develop vaccines for autoimmune diseases, including diabetes. **(Medi-Mation Ltd./Photo Researchers, Inc.)**

blood sugar in diabetic mice. Further, nanoparticle displaying human diabetes–relevant complexes restored normal blood sugar levels in a humanized model of diabetes. The authors pointed out that only the disease-generated white blood cells responded to the therapy, so the treatment would be inconsequential in healthy individuals because it would not have nonspecific effects on the immune system.

The researchers say such nanovaccines might hold promise in chronic autoimmune diseases, such as multiple sclerosis, rheumatoid arthritis, and others.

CHAPTER 2

Controversies Concerning Autoimmune Diseases

The Hygiene Hypothesis Can Explain the Rise in Autoimmune Diseases

Rob Stein

In the following viewpoint Rob Stein maintains that the rising incidence of autoimmune diseases and allergies can be attributed to the "hygiene hypothesis." First proposed in 1989, the hygiene hypothesis blames the rise in autoimmune diseases and allergies on the aseptic nature of industrialized countries and the prevalence of antibiotics. According to the hypothesis, without real invaders to fight against, immune systems attack the body's own tissues, causing autoimmune diseases, or they respond inappropriately to ordinarily benign substances, causing allergies. According to Stein, the hygiene hypothesis is the best theory scientists have to explain what appear to be epidemics of autoimmune diseases and allergies. Stein is a national science reporter for the *Washington Post*, focusing on health and medicine.

First, asthma cases shot up, along with hay fever and other common allergic reactions, such as eczema. Then, pediatricians started seeing more children with food allergies. Now [in 2008], experts are increasingly convinced that a suspected jump in lupus, multiple

SOURCE: Rob Stein, "Immune Systems Increasingly on Attack," *Washington Post*, March 4, 2008. Reprinted with permission.

Photo on facing page. Some researchers say that environmental toxins, such as pesticides and chemical cleaners, are responsible for the increasing occurrence of autoimmune diseases. **(Susan Leavines/Photo Researchers, Inc.)**

sclerosis [MS] and other afflictions caused by misfiring immune systems is real.

Though the data are stronger for some diseases than others, and part of the increase may reflect better diagnoses, experts estimate that many allergies and immune-system diseases have doubled, tripled or even quadrupled in the last few decades, depending on the ailment and country. Some studies now indicate that more than half of the U.S. population has at least one allergy.

The cause remains the focus of intense debate and study, but some researchers suspect the concurrent trends all may have a common explanation rooted in aspects of modern living—including the "hygiene hypothesis" that blames growing up in increasingly sterile homes, changes in diet, air pollution, and possibly even obesity and increasingly sedentary lifestyles.

More Antiseptic Lives

"We have dramatically changed our lives in the last 50 years," said Fernando Martinez, who studies allergies at the University of Arizona. "We are exposed to more products. We have people with different backgrounds being exposed to different environments. We have made our lives more antiseptic, especially early in life. Our immune systems may grow differently as a result. And we may be paying a price for that."

Along with a flurry of research to confirm and explain the trends, scientists have also begun testing possible remedies. Some are feeding high-risk children gradually larger amounts of allergy-inducing foods, hoping to train the immune system not to overreact. Others are testing benign bacteria or parts of bacteria. Still others have patients with MS, colitis and related ailments swallow harmless parasitic worms to try to calm their bodies' misdirected defenses.

"If you look at the incidence of these diseases, a lot of them began to emerge and become much more common after parasitic worm diseases were eliminated from our environment," said Robert Summers of the University of Iowa, who is experimenting with whipworms. "We believe they have a profound symbiotic effect on developing and maintaining the immune system."

Although hay fever, eczema, asthma and food allergies seem quite different, they are all "allergic diseases" because they are caused by the immune system responding to substances that are ordinarily benign, such as pollen or peanuts. Autoimmune diseases also result from the body's defense mechanisms malfunctioning. But in these diseases, which include lupus, MS, Type 1 diabetes and inflammatory bowel disease, the immune system attacks parts of the body such as nerves, the pancreas or digestive tract.

"Overall, there is very little doubt that we have seen significant increases," said Syed Hasan Arshad of the David Hide Asthma and Allergy Centre in England, who focuses on food allergies. "You can call it an epidemic. We're talking about millions of people and huge implications, both for health costs and quality of life. People miss work. Severe asthma can kill. Peanut allergies can kill. It does have huge implications all around. If it keeps increasing, where will it end?"

One reason that many researchers suspect something about modern living is to blame is that the increases show up largely in highly developed countries in Europe, North America and elsewhere, and have only started to rise in other countries as they have become more developed.

> **FAST FACT**
>
> Between 1988 and 2005 the incidence of Crohn's disease in northern France increased by 21 percent overall and by 48.5 percent in individuals younger than twenty, according to a study presented at the Digestive Disease Week conference in 2009.

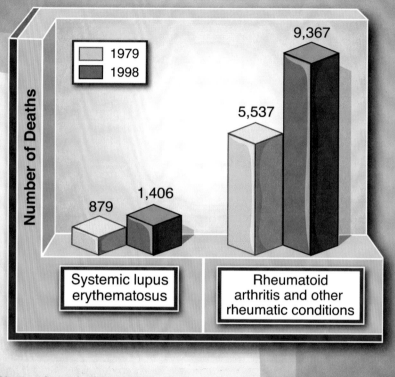

Lupus and Rheumatoid Arthritis, Increased US Deaths, 1979–1998

Number of Deaths

- 1979
- 1998

9,367

5,537

1,406

879

Systemic lupus erythematosus

Rheumatoid arthritis and other rheumatic conditions

Taken from: Centers for Disease Control and Prevention, *Morbidity and Mortality Weekly Report*, "Trends in Deaths from Systemic Lupus Erythematosus, United States, 1979–1998," May 3, 2002./J.J. Sacks et al. "Deaths from Arthritis and Other Rheumatic Conditions, United States, 1979–1998," *Journal of Rheumatology*, September 31, 2004.

"It's striking," said William Cookson of the Imperial College in London.

Less Busy Immune Systems

The leading theory to explain the phenomenon holds that as modern medicine beats back bacterial, viral and parasitic diseases that have long plagued humanity, immune systems may fail to learn how to differentiate between real threats and benign invaders, such as ragweed pollen or food. Or perhaps because they are not busy fighting real threats, they overreact or even turn on the body's own tissues.

"Our immune systems are much less busy," said Jean-Francois Bach of the French Academy of Sciences, "and so have much more strong responses to much weaker stimuli, triggering allergies and autoimmune diseases."

Several lines of evidence support the theory. Children raised with pets or older siblings are less likely to develop allergies, possibly because they are exposed to more microbes. But perhaps the strongest evidence comes from studies comparing thousands of people who grew up on farms in Europe to those who lived in less rural settings. Those reared on farms were one-tenth as likely to develop diseases such as asthma and hay fever.

"The data are very strong," said Erika von Mutius of the Ludwig-Maximilians University in Munich. "If kids have all sorts of exposures on the farm by being in the stables a lot, close to the animals and the grasses, and drinking cow's milk from their own farm, that seems to confer protection."

The theory has also gained support from a variety of animal studies. One, for example, found that rats bred in a sterile laboratory had far more sensitive immune systems than those reared in the wild, where they were exposed to infections, microorganisms and parasites.

"It's sort of a smoking gun of the hygiene hypothesis," said William Parker of Duke University.

Fewer Regulatory T Cells

Researchers believe the lack of exposure to potential threats early in life leaves the immune system with fewer command-and-control cells known as regulatory T cells, making the system more likely to overreact or run wild.

"If you live in a very clean society, you're not going to have a lot of regulatory T cells," Parker said.

While the evidence for the hygiene theory is accumulating, many say it remains far from proven.

"That theory is so full of holes that it's clearly not the whole story," said Robert Wood of the Johns Hopkins School of Medicine.

It does not explain, for example, the rise in asthma, since that disease occurs much more commonly in poor, inner-city areas where children are exposed to more cockroaches and rodents that may trigger it, Wood and others said.

Several alternative theories have been presented. Some researchers blame exposure to fine particles in air pollution, which may give the immune system more of a hair trigger, especially in genetically predisposed individuals. Others say obesity and a sedentary lifestyle may play a role. Still others wonder whether eating more processed food or foods processed in different ways, or changes in the balance of certain vitamins that can affect the immune system, such as vitamins C and E and fish oil, are a factor.

"Cleaning up the food we eat has actually changed what we're eating," said Thomas Platts-Mills of the University of Virginia.

Genetic Predisposition

But many researchers believe the hygiene hypothesis is the strongest, and that the reason one person develops asthma instead of hay fever or eczema or lupus or MS is because of a genetic predisposition.

"We believe it's about half and half," Cookson said. "You need environmental factors and you need genetic susceptibility as well."

Some researchers have begun to try to identify specific genes that may be involved, as well as specific components of bacteria or other pathogens that might be used to train immune systems to respond appropriately.

"If we could mimic what is happening in these farm environments, we could protect children and prevent asthma, allergies and other diseases," von Mutius said.

Some researchers are trying to help people who are at risk for allergies or already ill with autoimmune diseases.

With new research suggesting that food allergies may be occurring earlier in life and lasting longer, several small studies have been done or are underway in which children at risk for milk, egg and peanut allergies are given increasing amounts of those foods, beginning with tiny doses, to try to train the immune system.

"I'm very encouraged," said Wesley Burks, a professor of pediatrics at Duke who has done some of the studies. "I'm hopeful that in five years, there may be some type of therapy from this."

Parasitic Worms

Another promising line of research involves giving patients microscopic parasitic worms to try to tamp down the immune system.

"We've seen rather dramatic improvements in patients' conditions," said Summers of the University of Iowa, who has treated more than 100 people with Crohn's

A pig worm, an intestinal parasitic worm, is shown here. Researchers say that multiple sclerosis patients who had intestinal pig worm parasites fared better than those who did not. (**Dr. Keith Wheeler/ Photo Researchers, Inc.**

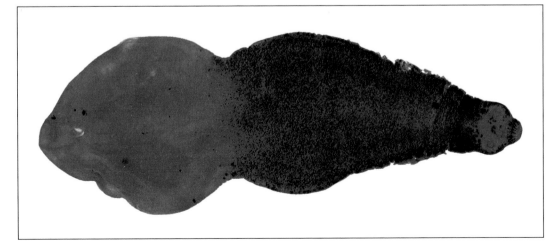

disease or ulcerative colitis by giving them parasitic worms that infect pigs but are harmless to humans. "We're not claiming that this is a cure, but we saw a very dramatic improvement. Some patients went into complete remission."

Doctors in Argentina reported last year that MS patients who had intestinal parasites fared better than those who did not, and researchers at the University of Wisconsin are planning to launch another study as early as next month testing pig worms in 20 patients with the disease.

"We hope to show whether this treatment has promise and is worth exploring further in a larger study," said John O. Fleming, a professor of neurology who is leading the effort.

The Rise in Autoimmune Diseases Can Be Blamed on Environmental Toxins

AlterNet, interview with Donna Jackson Nakazawa

In the following viewpoint Donna Jackson Nakazawa contends that environmental toxins are causing an epidemic of autoimmune diseases. In an interview with the website *AlterNet*, Nakazawa argues that people in industrialized countries are exposed to a plethora of immune system antagonists, from pesticides and heavy metals to food additives and bacterial and viral pathogens. She says this soup of toxins and chemicals is overburdening many people's immune systems, causing them to go awry and attack the body itself. Nakazawa wants to raise the public's awareness of autoimmune diseases and the link to environmental toxins. Nakazawa is the author of the 2008 book *The Autoimmune Epidemic: Bodies Gone Haywire in a World Out of Balance.* The *AlterNet* website is a program of the Independent Media Institute, a nonprofit organization that empowers people with independent journalism, information, and media tools.

*A*lternet: *In your book you say that the number of people suffering from autoimmune diseases such as lupus, multiple sclerosis and type 1 diabetes has skyrocketed—more than doubling in the last three decades. Yet we hear very little about this epidemic. Why?*

Donna Jackson Nakazawa: Lupus, multiple sclerosis, type 1 diabetes and rheumatoid arthritis are just a few of the more common types of autoimmune disease, but in fact there are nearly a hundred other known autoimmune diseases. One in 12 people—and one in 9 women—has an autoimmune disease. That's nearly 24 million Americans. Yet even though autoimmune diseases afflict more than double the number of people who have cancer, and a woman is 8 times more likely to have an autoimmune disease than breast cancer, 90 percent of Americans say they can't name a single autoimmune disease. That's because people just don't know that many painful and life-altering disorders that increasingly afflict so many of their friends and family members today are autoimmune in nature; the body's immune system, which is meant to protect us, is mistakenly attacking the body's own organs and systems.

We also don't hear much about these diseases because the exact process by which our immune system turns from friend to foe was, for many decades, the black box of modern science. Until the late 1970s scientists didn't even agree that the body could turn on itself, much less why. It's only in the last ten years that scientists have been able to show in the lab exactly how the immune system, when it's overwhelmed by foreign invaders such as chemicals and viruses, can go haywire and destroy our own tissue and organs in acts we might think of as "friendly fire." The fact that these diseases have been difficult for the medical community to understand means that even today [in 2008] getting a

FAST FACT

People who start smoking before age seventeen may increase their risk for developing multiple sclerosis, according to a study presented at the American Academy of Neurology's annual meeting in 2009.

correct diagnosis can be very difficult. Most people who have an autoimmune disease see six doctors over four years before they get a diagnosis. One patient suffering from severe muscle fatigue and disabling weakness was told by a doctor she'd seen eight times: "We've given you every test known to man except for an autopsy. Would you like one of those too?" It was five years before she got a diagnosis of myasthenia gravis. The medical establishment often lacks a full understanding as to how to diagnose these diseases, dismisses women who complain of symptoms, and often has little to offer in the way of effective treatment. So one reason autoimmune diseases are not on our radar screens is that these diseases were, for many decades, mysterious and not well understood.

"Global Warming of Women's Health"

Another reason, I suspect, is that on some level we don't want to face the facts. Rates of these diseases have doubled and tripled in industrialized countries around the world over the past three decades. The top scientists I interviewed for my book [*The Autoimmune Epidemic*] agree that something in our environment—something far beyond a better ability to diagnose these diseases—is causing this health crisis. They are convinced that the cause of this epidemic—which is world-wide, by the way—lies primarily in our environment and in all the toxins, pesticides, heavy metals and chemicals that have become a part of our everyday living. We all carry a "body burden" of toxins in our bloodstream, even babies. Several studies show that chemicals commonly used in household cleaners, cosmetics and furniture are present in infant fetal cord blood. This doesn't sound healthy, does it? But even if we agree that this soup of chemicals within us is harmful, what do we do about it? Talking about the autoimmune epidemic is a bit like talking about global warming before the movie *An Inconvenient Truth* was released. For the longest time, we couldn't see, or didn't want to see, that the smallest rise in temperature would melt the polar ice caps. Likewise, we don't want to know that the ways we're polluting our environment are also harming our bodies and our immune cells. In the international medical world, the scientists who study autoimmune disease call this epidemic "the global warming of women's health." Yet the reality that the environment plays a major role in triggering these diseases hasn't yet trickled down to the rest of the population.

You coin the term "autogen" to describe the agents that trigger autoimmune disease. What are some examples of autogens?

There are thousands of probable autogens we have not yet studied. Eighty thousand chemicals have been approved for use in our environment. Every year 1700 new chemicals are approved—that's an average of five a day. Have scientists studied the effects on our bodies of all these chemicals? No. However, those chemicals that have been researched—in occupational studies and in studies of lab animals—have been shown to play a role in triggering autoimmune reactions. For example, mice exposed to pesticides—at levels four-fold lower than the level set as acceptable for humans by the EPA [Environmental Protection Agency]—are more susceptible to getting lupus than control mice. Mice that absorb low doses of trichloroethylene (TCE)—a chemical used in industrial degreasers, dry-cleaning, household paint thinners, glues and adhesives—at levels deemed safe by the EPA, and equal to what a factory worker today might encounter, quickly develop autoimmune hepatitis. And low doses of perfluorooctanoic acid, a breakdown chemical of Teflon that can be found in 96 percent of humans tested for it, impair the development of a proper immune system in rats.

We know from occupational studies in humans that these chemicals impair our immune systems in dangerous ways. In 2007, scientists from the National Institutes of Health announced—after studying 300,000 death cer-

Lupus Is Associated with Occupational Exposure to Mercury, Pesticides, or Solvents

An "odds ratio" is a way to compare the probability of an event occurring in two different groups. Odds ratios greater than one imply that the event is more likely to occur.

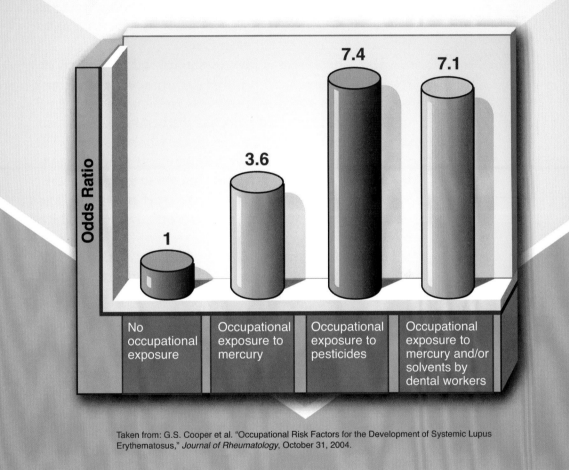

Taken from: G.S. Cooper et al. "Occupational Risk Factors for the Development of Systemic Lupus Erythematosus," *Journal of Rheumatology*, October 31, 2004.

tificates in 26 states over a 14-year period—that those who worked with pesticides, textiles, hand painting, solvents (such as TCE), benzene, asbestos, and other compounds were significantly more likely to die from an autoimmune disease than people who were not exposed. Other recent studies show links between working with solvents, silica dust, asbestos, PCBs [polychlorinated biphenyls] and vinyl chloride and a greater likelihood of developing autoimmune disease.

The Barrel Effect

But not everyone who is exposed to these autogens comes down with a disease. So, why do some people get an autoimmune disease and not others?

That's because of a phenomenon I call the "barrel effect." Each person, with his or her unique genetic composition, is exposed to a myriad combination and level of autogens depending on what they encounter in their day-to-day lives through the air they breathe and what they come into contact with through their skin. This toxic stew consists not only of chemicals and heavy metals, but additives in our highly processed diet and viruses and bacterial agents to which we're exposed—all of which combine to impact our immune system. Chronic stress, which releases cortisol into our body, also plays a role in triggering these diseases as do women's reproductive hormones—which is why women are three times more likely than men to come down with an autoimmune disease. As long as your barrel is less than full, however, your immune system is still able to deal with what it confronts every day. But once the immune system becomes overburdened it can begin to send misread signals, causing the immune system to make costly mistakes and attack the body itself. Unfortunately in modern life we've created a perfect storm of factors—a plethora of chemicals, heavy metals, processed food additives, viral hits and stressors—for today's autoimmune epidemic to take hold. So much of what we encounter in twenty-first century life is causing our barrel to fill to the brim—and spill over. At that point, disease strikes.

Is it only people with a genetic predisposition who are vulnerable to this "barrel effect"?

No. Researchers have found that anyone can be susceptible. Whether or not you get an autoimmune disease depends on how many of these triggers you've been exposed to over your lifetime—or how full your barrel is. People with a genetic predisposition—for example, if you have a close relative who has an autoimmune disease, you may be genetically inclined that way—may be more vulnerable, but anyone whose immune system is overtaxed or over-stimulated can get sick.

Autoimmune Clusters

You talk about "clusters" of autoimmune diseases in your book. For example, in Buffalo, NY, in a small neighborhood surrounding known toxic waste sites, an unusually high number of people have developed lupus. And yet, [government environmental agencies are] doubtful that there's a link. Why is that?

Clusters are hugely controversial in part because our scientific criteria for proving that exposure A caused disease B in a community are extremely difficult to meet.

A sign warns fishers about mercury in bass in the Florida Everglades. Researchers say heavy metals are among the leading causes of autoimmune diseases. (Jack Dermind/Photo Researchers, Inc.)

WARNING
HEALTH HAZARD

DO NOT EAT MORE THAN ONE BASS
PER WEEK PER ADULT DUE TO
HIGH MERCURY CONTENT

CHILDREN & PREGNANT WOMEN
SHOULD NOT EAT BASS

NPS-EVER

Autoimmune diseases take years to appear after exposure, and communities are often constantly changing. People move, or die, or their disease is never properly diagnosed. How can we prove, with all these variables, that a toxic exposure in an area caused a group of people to fall ill with a specific set of diseases? Moreover, so much toxic waste exists everywhere, how can we definitively compare what autoimmune disease rates might be in a non-chemically laden area with those in a highly contaminated area when such clear-cut lines rarely exist in the cities and suburbs where we live? So it's very difficult.

Nevertheless, autoimmune clusters have been shown to exist near toxic waste sites in Buffalo, New York; El Paso, Texas; and Morrison, Illinois, and its environs. Many more are being investigated, including in Anniston, Alabama, where investigators funded by the Agency for Toxic Substances and Disease Registry are conducting studies to determine whether high rates of autoimmune disease in the area are linked to an industrial manufacturing site where most of the PCBs in the United States were once manufactured and dumped. From Anniston to Buffalo we live in an increasingly complex sea of autogenic agents.

Still, we say we can't "prove" that chemicals are impairing the human immune system. Meanwhile, European environmental policy uses the precautionary principle— an approach to public health that underscores preventing harm to human health before it happens. In June 2007, the European Union implemented legislation known as REACH (the Registration, Evaluation, Authorization and Restriction of Chemical Substances), which requires companies to develop safety data on 30,000 chemicals over the next decade, and places responsibility on the chemical industry to demonstrate the safety of their products. America lags far behind, without any precautionary guidelines regarding chemical use.

Obviously, political and economic considerations come into play here. There are over 1200 "superfund" sites around the U.S.—areas where deadly toxins are known to be seeping into the environment—and these have yet to be cleaned up. At about 10 percent of these sites, people are freely entering the area and being exposed directly to the hazardous waste. Unfortunately, the Environmental Protection Agency does not release information about how much it plans to spend to remediate these sites, when the area will be cleaned up or how long it will take.

You were twice paralyzed with the autoimmune disease Guillan Barré Syndrome during the writing of this book. How did you recover?

Most patients with an autoimmune disease go through terribly difficult times—or flare-ups—which can be quite serious. Getting through a downturn involves a combination of factors. If you know what can contribute to disease it's easier to know how you can help yourself. Months of grueling physical therapy, coupled with IVIG [intravenous immunoglobulin] treatments, helped me recover each time I was paralyzed. I also have had to be vigilant about what goes into my body and avoid coming into contact with things that might overstimulate my immune system. Dietary factors, use of household cleaners, emotional stress—these all have to be watched and managed. Also, we do a lot of hand washing in my home, especially when there are colds and flu going around, to minimize any viral hits to my immune system. Studies show that patients with an autoimmune disease also do better if they build a wellness plan that involves reducing stress hormones through a daily habit of meditation and whatever form of exercise they can tolerate. Studies show that autoimmune patients also do much better if they follow "the autoimmune diet," which means consuming foods that are anti-inflammatory.

Vaccines Play a Role in Causing Autoimmune Diseases

Yehuda Shoenfeld et al.

In the following viewpoint Yehuda Shoenfeld and his associates contend that vaccines can cause autoimmune diseases. Vaccines for rubella, mumps, and measles are among those cited by Shoenfeld and his colleagues as being associated with autoimmune diseases such as rheumatoid arthritis, lupus, and diabetes. The authors acknowledge that vaccinations have eradicated some diseases and prevented the deaths of many people. However, vaccinations may have adverse effects, the authors say, and those related to autoimmune diseases are the most serious of these. Shoenfeld heads the Center for Autoimmune Diseases at the Sheba Medical Center at Tel Aviv University in Israel.

Since 1796, when Edward Jenner inoculated cowpox material and prevented smallpox in 12 people, vaccination has been used as an indispensable tool against infectious diseases. In fact, it may be considered

SOURCE: Yehuda Shoenfeld et al. "The Mosaic of Autoimmunity: Hormonal and Environmental Factors Involved in Autoimmune Diseases—2008," *Israel Medical Association Journal*, vol. 10, January 2008, pp. 8–12. Reproduced by permission.

one of the greatest medical discoveries since it succeeded in totally eradicating some diseases around the world (plague and smallpox) and consequently improved the quality of life and survival of entire populations.

Vaccines' Adverse Effects

However, several adverse effects can ensue from the vaccination, ranging from local reactions to systemic side effects, such as fever, flu-like symptoms, gastrointestinal disorders and, in the last two to three decades, the most serious—autoimmune diseases. Considerable data have recently [in 2008] been gathered with regard to

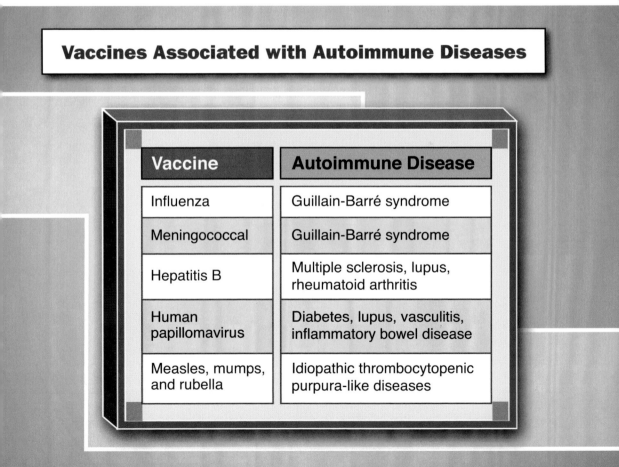

Vaccines Associated with Autoimmune Diseases

Vaccine	Autoimmune Disease
Influenza	Guillain-Barré syndrome
Meningococcal	Guillain-Barré syndrome
Hepatitis B	Multiple sclerosis, lupus, rheumatoid arthritis
Human papillomavirus	Diabetes, lupus, vasculitis, inflammatory bowel disease
Measles, mumps, and rubella	Idiopathic thrombocytopenic purpura-like diseases

Taken from: Hedi Orbach, Nancy Agmon-Levin, and Gisele Zandman-Goddard, "Vaccines and Autoimmune Diseases of the Adult," *Discovery Medicine*, February 4, 2010.

involvement of the immune system following vaccination, although its precise role has not been fully elucidated. Several authors have postulated that the autoimmunity process could be triggered or enhanced by vaccine immunogen content as well as by adjuvants, which are used to increase the immune reaction.

A common target for the occurrence of autoimmune complications is the central nervous system, with the appearance of demyelinating disorders [where the myelin sheaths covering nerves are damaged] such as multiple sclerosis, and other neurological conditions, e.g., Guillain-Barré syndrome and autism.

Other autoimmune diseases that may occur after vaccination include arthritis, rheumatoid arthritis, reactive arthritis, SLE [systemic lupus erythematosus],

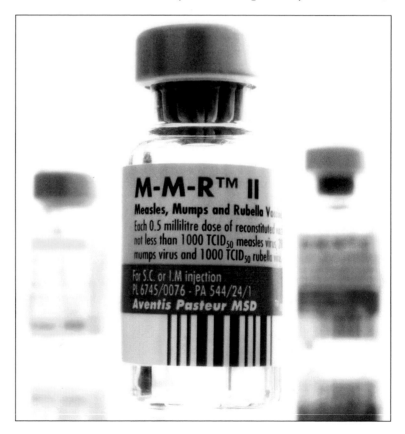

Research on the vaccine for measles, mumps, and rubella has found it to be associated with autoimmune diseases, such as arthritis, lupus, and diabetes. (Saturn Stills/Photo Researchers, Inc.)

diabetes mellitus, thrombocytopenia, vasculitis, Reiter's syndrome, dermatomyositis, and polyarteritis nodosa. Other vaccines reported to be associated with the onset of autoimmune disorders are the following: rubella, mumps and measles; influenza; diphtheria, pertussis and toxoid; typhoid; hepatitis A and B; tetanus; Meningococcus; Bacillus Calmette-Guerin; rabies; smallpox; and poliovirus vaccines (practically all types).

Vaccines and Autoimmunity

The relationship between vaccines and autoimmunity is bi-directional. On the one hand, vaccines prevent infectious conditions, and in turn prevent the development of an overt autoimmune disease which in some individuals is triggered by infections. On the other hand, many case reports and series that describe autoimmune diseases post-vaccination strongly suggest that vaccines can trigger autoimmunity.

It is important to emphasize that a temporal relationship between autoimmunity and a specific vaccine is not always apparent. This matter is complicated by the fact that one vaccine may cause more than one autoimmune phenomenon and, likewise, a particular immune process may be caused by more than one vaccine.

Appropriate epidemiological studies should be undertaken to confirm the case reports or series where familial or genetic risk factors for autoimmune conditions were found in many of the patients who developed autoimmune disturbances after vaccination. In this way, vaccination should be considered part of the mosaic of autoimmunity, in which abrogation of an infectious disease could concomitantly induce another autoimmune disease. In summary, throughout our lifetime the normal immune system walks a fine line between preserving normalcy and the development of autoimmune disease.

> **FAST FACT**
>
> In 1976 a national swine flu vaccination campaign was ended after the vaccine was linked with the development of Guillain-Barré syndrome, according to the Centers for Disease Control and Prevention.

It Is Not Certain That Vitamin D Can Help Prevent Autoimmune Diseases

Stephen Strauss

In the following viewpoint Stephen Strauss asserts that even though many people are calling vitamin D a wonder drug, it is not clear that it actually prevents autoimmune diseases. Strauss discusses a controversial new treatment for autoimmune diseases, called the Marshall Protocol, which advises patients to avoid vitamin D. The protocol is based on the theory that the vitamin stifles the body's ability to fight off certain pathogenic bacteria, which, according to the Marshall Protocol, are the true culprits in autoimmune diseases. Strauss thinks there are many problems with the Marshall Protocol, but he believes that it does illustrate the complexity of how vitamin D affects the body. Strauss contends that until this complexity is unraveled, the truth about vitamin D's role in autoimmune diseases remains uncertain. Strauss is a Canadian science and technology newspaper journalist and the author of several books.

SOURCE: Stephen Strauss, "Vitamin D: Not a Simple Case of Cause and Effect," CBC News, October 27, 2008. Reproduced by permission of the author.

I swear I didn't plan to grow up and become a vitamin D cowboy, but here I am, again galloping into the vitamin corral, again trying to get an intellectual rope around the question of whether the "sunshine vitamin" really is medicine's next clap-hands-hosanna—or not.

The Marshall Protocol Versus "Vitamin D Is Good for You" Debate

The context for this reflection are four presentations about what has come to be known as the Marshall Protocol made in September [2003] in Portugal at the 6th International Congress on Autoimmunity. In a 21st-century world in which the talk everywhere seems to be that taking much, much more vitamin D—five to 10 times the present recommended dosage—is needed if humans in northern and far southern countries are to curtail cancers and slack the growth of autoimmune diseases, the Marshall presenters reached a 180-degree, U-turn of a conclusion.

Looking at more than 1,000 people with a host of autoimmune and related diseases, the researchers said that—when combined with a particular drug treatment program—people who consciously tried not to take vitamin D and stayed out of the sun showed an often-dramatic reduction in symptoms. Dramatic means a reduction of 81 per cent in symptoms for people suffering from conditions ranging from Type 2 diabetes, to rheumatoid arthritis, to multiple sclerosis, Lyme disease and Crohn's disease.

One drug in the protocol is called olmesartan, a medication currently approved for high blood pressure and vitamin-D-reduction use in certain diseases, and the others are low doses of certain antibiotics.

What is the rationale for this treatment? A very, very complicated body biology.

Marshall Protocol initiator Trevor Marshall later told me that it is scientifically accepted that forms of vitamin

Number of Patients Avoiding Vitamin D Reporting Symptom Improvement by Diagnosis

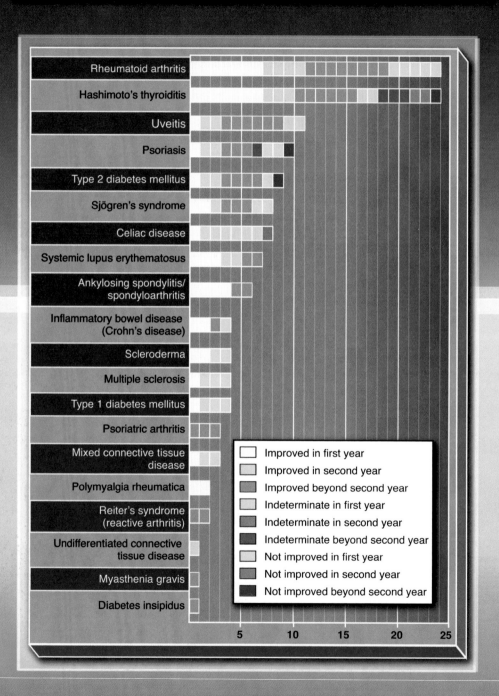

Taken from: Tom Perez, "Presentation—Bacteria Induced Vitamin D Receptor Dysfunction in Autoimmune Disease," Sixth International Congress on Autoimmunity, September 11, 2008.

D act as a steroid that, among other things, modulates the body's immune responses. In his model, certain kinds of bacteria invade the white cells that the body uses to fight and destroy foreign invaders. The compromised cells respond by generating inflammation. The inflammation ends up throwing off the body's ability to effectively use vitamin D to ramp up and dampen down immune responses. The form of vitamin D that is usually measured to determine deficiency has to be converted to another active form and, without that conversion, according to Marshall, the vitamin D supplements actually dampen down the immune system.

This immune suppression allows the bacteria inside the white cells to multiply. As they do, the inflammation that Marshall sees lying at the root of autoimmune diseases increases and with that, another round of inflammation is generated.

The whole Marshall Protocol debate is clearly an example of the new world where people are exposed to massive amounts of contentious health information on the Internet. This raises the question of how this dispute can be laid out for the unwary. The best place I have found is that often-belittled source of information, Wikipedia. The Wikipedia article itself is of little interest, but what is fascinating is the note that directs readers of the online encyclopedia to what didn't get in, and why.

In the protocol, the banning of vitamin D prevents the imbalance from self-perpetuating; the olmesartan returns the immune system response to its normal state, so that the antibiotics can kill the rogue bacteria.

What does this mean for the more-vitamin-D-is-good-for-you debate?

In a paper entitled "Vitamin D Discovery Outpaces FDA Decision-Making," which Marshall published last year [2007] in the peer reviewed journal *BioEssays*, he wrote the following immensely provocative few sentences: "For half a century, medical science has been noting

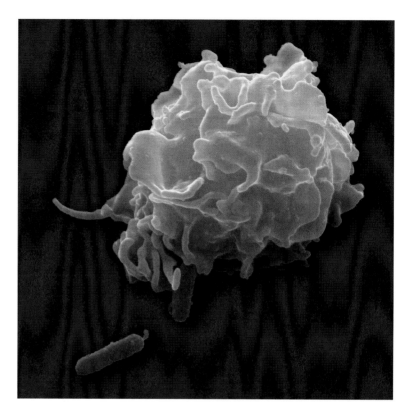

An electron micrograph shows a white blood cell engulfing a pathogenic bacteria (pink). The Marshall Protocol is based on the theory that some forms of vitamin D stifle the body's ability to fight off certain pathogenic bacteria, which the protocol's proponents say are the true cause of autoimmune diseases. (Juergen Berger/Photo Researchers, Inc.)

the association between vitamin D serum levels and disease. What developed has been a concept of 'vitamin D deficiency' based solely on the notion that 'low' vitamin D serum levels somehow cause disease processes. But this ignores the alternative hypothesis—that the disease processes themselves regulate the vitamin D metabolism—that the observed 'low' values of vitamin D in disease are a result of the disease process, not the cause."

Oof. The supposed cause is the really an effect. Oof.

Marshall Protocol Weaknesses

I report this to you and then almost as quickly want to rein back on what I have told you. The Marshall Protocol is not your classic double-blind/don't tell patients who is getting antibiotics and olmesartan and who isn't sort of thing. Everyone who enrolls, with their doctor's approval, gets the drugs. There is no part of the study in which people are encouraged to go into the sun or take more vitamin D. The people who went into the study were all very sick, "at the end of their ropes," Marshall says, and were looking for something, anything, to make their pain-filled lives better.

Moreover, the presenters generally had rather unconventional backgrounds. Marshall is a PhD electrical engineer who has gotten heavily involved with computer simulations of various sorts, and his PhD thesis was entitled *Modelling and Simulation in Diabetes Care*. Another was a retired captain in the Commission Corps of the U.S. Public Health Services who worked in the Food and Drug Administration. And yet another had a BA in biology and wrote her senior thesis on the Marshall Protocol.

Most seem to have one or another of the conditions which the treatment is designed to cure.

That is to say they are, as they say in French, parti pris [having a preconceived opinion]. They really want the treatment to work because they really need it to work in their lives. This means that the fabled placebo effect, with its oft times 30 per cent improvement level, may be part of what is going on.

As well, Marshall doesn't plan to have the protocol's results submitted to a peer-reviewed journal for publication. He is just going to speak at meetings. Why? He complains about the medical community's inability to appreciate the new biochemistry of the genes and its subsequent unwillingness to move beyond the double-blind study.

"Our studies were designed to make breakthroughs, not to fit into paradigms that big medicine was capable of understanding," he tells me. "I think it is highly unlikely we will be publishing our study results. I think others will replicate our work and they will publish."

Or not. Maybe what others' published research will show is that Marshall is wrong—something peer review would let him see today.

And it is also fair to say that much of the conventional scientific community thinks Marshall's science—what he personally does is generate computer simulations of how cells and proteins might interact—is somewhere between plain wrong and awfully loony. "His paper really ignored large swatches of literature on vitamin D functions. There is nothing in what he has said or published that modifies my views about how vitamin D works," is how John White, a molecular geneticist at McGill University who late last year published an extensive piece in *Scientific American* about vitamin D and its effect on cells, views Marshall's research.

What is particularly lacking is "wet" data—that is, actual experiments with cells and vitamin D that show that Marshall's computer-based theories are correct.

Quite damning in this regard, White will soon submit for publication an experiment which contradicts some of Marshall's computer-based theories of how the body processes vitamin D.

Complexity and Uncertainty

Now my intellectual horse rears up another time. However flawed it may turn out to be, at least the Marshall Protocol presents a clear biochemical pathway that explains what happens in diseases and how vitamin D affects the body.

This is in clear contrast to those who advocate taking much greater amounts of vitamin D. They haven't clearly defined the mechanisms by which the vitamin can cure you or prevent a disease from occurring. And there is a reason for this. The more we know about vitamin D, the more complicated its actions in the body seem. White reported in his *Scientific American* paper that at least 1,000 genes are regulated by 1,25 D, the metabolically active form of the vitamin.

Even this is likely a low estimate of its ultimate effect. White writes in the same paper that many other genes are influenced by vitamin D activity.

What this suggests is that whatever happens with vitamin D and disease, the process is likely extremely complicated. And thus increasing dosage is something one wants to do with great, great care. This is not a world of a cause and an effect; this is a body planet where a multiplicity of disease causes and a multiplicity of medicine effects are occurring.

With this in mind, White, who publicly admits that he now takes 4,000 international units of the vitamin daily in winter instead of Health Canada's presently recommended 200, also preaches caution.

"I am very concerned people are going to have the expectation that vitamin D will cure everything—and it will not," he tells me with high seriousness. "You have to keep a certain distance and be critical here, and I would argue that some vitamin D proponents are just as guilty [as Marshall], but in the other direction. Taking vitamin D doesn't mean that all of a sudden no one is . . . ever going to get cancer, no one is ever going to get multiple sclerosis anymore, etc, etc."

And with that, my intellectual horse . . . rears up a final time and—in its still uncertain search for the truth about vitamin D and disease—gallops off in all directions.

> ## FAST FACT
>
> According to the International and American Associations of Clinical Nutritionists, twenty minutes of exposure to sunlight of the correct wavelength generates about 20,000 international units (IUs) of vitamin D in a healthy adult.

Challenging the Immune System Is Important for Health

William Meller

In the following excerpt from his book *Evolution Rx*, William Meller asserts that autoimmune diseases and allergies are the result of unchallenged immune systems. Meller describes how during the Stone Age the immune system protected humans from a multitude of worms, germs, and other "creepy crawlies" to which humans were constantly exposed. In fact, he asserts, evidence exists that the presence of intestinal parasites is linked to a lower incidence of autoimmune diseases. As human conditions have gotten cleaner and more aseptic, the immune system has gone awry, like a warrior looking for a fight, and caused allergies and autoimmune diseases. Meller is hopeful that science will one day find effective treatments for autoimmune diseases and allergies. Until then he says to stay away from immune system supplements, or other alternative treatments, which he calls quackery. Meller also advises people to expose their immune systems to a multitude of challenges in the natural world. Meller is an internal medicine physician and a practitioner of evolutionary medicine, which applies modern evolutionary theory to understanding health and disease.

You may remember your grandmother saying, "You eat a peck of dirt before you die." Perhaps she was reassuring you, as she brushed off a slice of toast that had dropped to the floor, that no harm would come to you by eating it. Nowadays this bit of wisdom has given way to the "three-second rule," which tells us to avoid eating anything that's been on the floor longer than that. How careful do we really need to be?

Imagine how dirty you'd get on a camping trip that lasted a million years. No showers, no soap, no concept of cleanliness other than picking your teeth with a twig after meals. Stone Age people rarely bathed. Every night they slept in the dirt or on a pile of leaves. Rocks, bones, and sticks served as tables and cutlery. They wasted little energy cleaning their children.

Every bite of food they ate—whether berry, root, bug, or leaf—was garnished with grit. They ate meat raw, partially cooked, or nearly rotten, ingesting parasites and worms as part of the daily fare. Many plant foods were so tough they had to be ground into mush between stones, which added a heavy seasoning of microbes and soil.

Despite all this dirt, early humans prospered nicely. Sticks for digging and lethal stone points helped broaden their diet by adding roots and larger game. Following their prey north to cooler climates, they wore animal skins to keep warm, even though those garments harbored a menagerie of creepy crawlies. Much later they domesticated cattle and pets along with an exotic menagerie of shared parasites. Our ancestors' skin, hair, and intestines provided a happy home for fungi, viruses, and bacteria. Any concept of cleanliness lay far in the future.

In short, this early era of humankind might better be known as the Dirt Age. Our forebears lived and died in a grubby world. Bathing was not even a concept until recent millennia and then emerged as a ritual practiced mostly on sacred occasions, more often for spiritual than for bodily cleansing.

Because they lived in filth, you'd think these cave dwellers and nomads were sick all the time. Actually, no.

To thrive on a diet of dirty water and contaminated food, our ancestors evolved potent defenses to disarm germs, neutralize toxins, and repel parasites. While the fossil record overflows with evidence of broken bones and nutritional challenges, our very existence confirms the evolutionary success of our ancestors in the long struggle against the tiniest of predators.

But there's a catch. The same immune system that has defended us so ably since the Stone Age appears to be veering off the mark in modern times. Allergies appear when our immunity takes aim at innocent bystanders like pollen or pets. In the mysterious conditions known as autoimmune diseases, our own immune systems target our properly working joints, nerves, and organs.

Are Our Immune Systems Failing Us?

"Why is my immune system so weak?" patients often ask me. "I'm always getting sick. My immunity must be shot!"

Our immune systems are not fragile things that fall apart with the first sniffle of a cold or flush of the flu. . . . The very symptoms we suffer when sick—chills, fever, sweating, phlegm, cough, loss of appetite, and lethargy— signal that our bodies are hard at work making life unpleasant for these ancient invaders. Even catching two or three colds in a year doesn't mean our bodies are falling apart. It's just a run of bad luck.

Our immune systems very rarely break down, except when we starve, undergo intensive chemotherapy, or face an immune-system assassin such as HIV. These are life-threatening emergencies, not occasions to take an alleged immune "stimulant."

The threat of imminent immune system collapse is the calling card of quackery. Just think of how many health-food products, yoga postures, and alternative therapies claim to stimulate immune function to fend off infections, cancer, and even old age.

Us Against Them

Immunity has been likened to a sixth sense. While the survival benefits of sight and smell are obvious, we wouldn't last long without our invisible immune system ever on the prowl, detecting our unseen enemies and protecting us from the ravages of these tiny living things that seek to invade us and multiply.

Although the immune system goes about its business with bustling efficiency, it is usually a silent ally. For one thing, it's not like an organ or a limb that we can see or feel with our hands. It's made of cells and proteins scattered throughout the body—in the blood, lymph nodes, bone marrow, spleen, and even appendix.

At its most basic, the immune system is made up of white blood cells and the tissues that make and harbor them. Red blood cells do the light lifting, carrying oxygen to our tissues, while white blood cells do all the dirty work. They oversee the cleanup of injured tissue, the healing of wounds, and the removal of cancerous cells. Important tasks, indeed.

The immune system is the body's homeland security. Some immune cells stand guard in the skin and gut, on the lookout for everyday invaders. Others patrol constantly, ready to call out a SWAT team of killer cells when a germ makes it through our first defenses. Still others haul the weakened offenders to nearby lymph nodes. These nodes swell, causing, for example, the tender lumps we feel under the jaw when we have a sore throat.

Then come the antibodies. These are highly specific proteins programmed to recognize and remember a specific bacteria or virus forever. They are the memory of the immune system, always on the lookout for repeat offenders.

Our immune system never rests. In the mouth and gut it neutralizes germs that hitchhike in on food. In the lungs it screens the air we breathe. In the skin it wards off invaders trying to enter through dirty cuts and scrapes.

The fact that we get so few infections, despite countless daily exposure, testifies to the vigilance of our immune forces.

Rather than being weak, it is far more common today that our immune system is overactive. The fine tuning that kept this essential defense in balance in the Stone Age has gone haywire in modern times. Instead of snatching up invading viruses and bacteria, they often grab a scrap of plant pollen, animal dander, or even one of our own cells and attack it as if it were harmful to us.

This is what we call an allergy or an autoimmune disease. . . .

The Immune Response to Parasites

The disconnect between our ancient immune systems and today's overscrubbed lifestyle . . . appears in a lineup of devastating new conditions known as *autoimmune diseases*. This group is the rogue's gallery of immunity gone awry—rheumatoid arthritis, lupus, multiple sclerosis (MS), scleroderma, Crohn's disease, celiac disease, Graves' disease, and type 1 diabetes.

To trace the missing link between our evolutionary past and these modern maladies, remember our Stone Age family. While Mom gathered berries, her babies crawled around naked in the dirt. Just like toddlers today, they put everything into their mouths. The first time a little bundle of joy was set down on the dirt floor of a cave or left to squirm in the grass, that baby was exposed to a world of microbes, parasites, and worms—and swallowed them all. And these were tough, well-adapted intestinal worms that specialized in setting up shop inside of us, not the friendly ones we use to catch bass.

Parasitic intestinal worms are not simpleminded creatures like bacteria and viruses. They are highly evolved organisms with their own internal organs, sex lives, and chemical weapons that they can turn on us. In their ongoing challenge of evading our immune system, what could be better than to shut down our immune attacks on them? The best offense is to take out the other guy's defense.

Because parasites are so large and well defended, our immune response shifted long ago from trying to kill them to trying to control their numbers. We are still not very good at it. Even today, people in the developing world often harbor up to six types of intestinal parasites, all living in a kind of armed internal harmony.

On the other hand, these same infested people have far fewer autoimmune diseases than we do. In the developed world, most of us *never* have any worms living in us, but roughly 6 percent of the population is diagnosed with an autoimmune disease at some point in their lives. Could there be a connection?

Autoimmune diseases are ones in which our own immune systems take aim at parts of our bodies. The prime culprits in these ailments are auto-antibodies—antibodies misdirected at our own tissue. They can attack almost any tissue in the body, including the pancreas (type 1 diabetes), cartilage (rheumatoid arthritis), connective tissue (lupus), nervous system (MS), skin (scleroderma), gut (Crohn's and celiac disease), and thyroid (Graves' disease).

Medicine has struggled to understand and treat some 40 known or suspected autoimmune diseases since they were first discovered early in the 20th century. We can turn down autoimmunity with corticosteroids and other powerful drugs but risk suppressing the rest of the immune system, which fights infections and even cancer in its early stages.

It might seem nonsensical that our own immune troops would rebel against us, but an evolutionary perspective offers powerful insight into the origin and new treatments for these conditions.

FAST FACT

According to a 2002 Harris Poll, 59 percent of Americans mistakenly believe that vitamins, minerals, and other food supplements must be approved by a government agency like the Food and Drug Administration before they can be sold to the public.

Possible Benefits of Intestinal Parasites

One arm of the immune system, our antibodies, reacts quickly to harmful bacteria and viruses. This gang shoots fast and straight without asking questions. Only a few viruses, notably chickenpox and herpes, manage to evade complete removal.

The other limb of the immune system helps pursue parasites and worms, a far more complicated task. These nasties have gotten very good at hiding out within our bodies. One of their tricks is to release chemicals that suppress our immune response. Modern medicine has actually borrowed some of these compounds, such as the drug Tacrolimus, which is made from a fungus and is used to inhibit the rejection of transplanted organs.

The evolutionary lesson we are learning is that our immune systems expect to be challenged in this way. Until recently we *always* had parasites within us. What's unusual is our modern condition: having no parasites in our midst. Our immune forces now operate without the influence of those ancient modulators—like loaded guns with the safety off and no clear and present threat. The result is that they mistakenly target our body's own tissues.

There is good evidence that specific worms calm our immune response and suppress inflammation. Joel Weinstock, now at Tufts University, found that patients in the developing world who are treated to remove worms develop colitis and other inflammatory bowel diseases approximately 10 years later at rates similar to those seen in Western societies.

Knowing that pig farmers are often infected with a common pig worm with no apparent side effects, Weinstock, in 2005, gave specific doses of the worms' eggs to patients with Crohn's disease, an intestinal autoimmune disease. Of the 29 patients treated, 21 went into complete remission. In another study of patients with ulcerative colitis, 13 of 30 patients improved, compared to 4 in the control group. Similar studies are now under way in patients with multiple sclerosis, asthma, food allergies, and hay fever.

Celiac Disease

A similar line of evolutionary research accounts for the autoimmune disease known as celiac disease, sprue, or gluten enteropathy. Affecting about 1 percent of people in Western societies, sprue is an antibody reaction against gluten, one of the principal proteins in wheat seeds. Wheat evolved this protein ages ago to keep its precious seeds from being eaten—by mammals like us.

Over the thousands of years humans have been eating wheat, most evolved an ability to digest gluten. But some people make an antibody that, although it is directed against gluten, also attacks the lining of their own small intestine—another case of mistaken identity. The intestine becomes inflamed, swollen, and less effective at

Celiac disease is an antibody reaction against wheat gluten. The mucosa in the small intestine becomes compressed and develops a mosaic-like pattern, shown here. The cause is genetic. **(Biophoto Associates/ Photo Researchers, Inc.)**

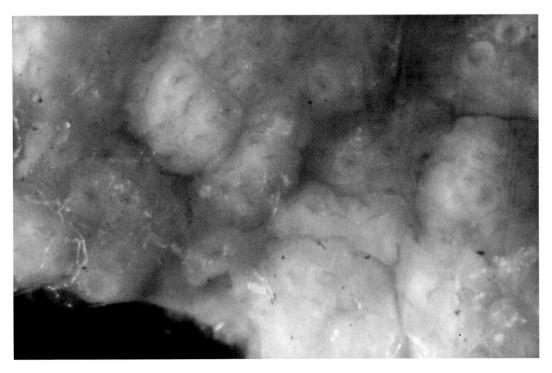

absorbing essential nutrients. The result is diarrhea, malnutrition, and no end of discomfort.

It is important to realize that this is not an allergy to gluten but a misguided antibody reacting against part of our own intestine. The treatment is straightforward, if not easy to carry out. Avoid wheat. Anyone who has tried this knows very well how many packaged, processed, and fast foods contain this common grain.

Predisposition for celiac disease is genetic, but the age at which a child is exposed to wheat proteins influences the outcome. Several studies show that longer breast-feeding and withholding wheat products until after 6 months of age protect against developing sprue later in life.

As often happens when Western medicine is ineffective, the absence of a quick and sure cure for allergies and autoimmunity opens the door to an onslaught of alternative health practices promising relief. When doctors can't help, some of us want to believe that massage or crystals, herbs or supplements, will. But be careful. Widely advertised "immune stimulants" claim to do the exact opposite of what we need to do to control allergies and autoimmune diseases. We need to quiet the inappropriate immune response, not stimulate it.

Immune Systems Should Be Challenged

Evolutionary medicine recognizes that our immune systems are powerful today because of the filthy conditions endured by our ancestors. Because our intestines evolved expecting to harbor parasites, we suffer autoimmunity in their absence. Because our respiratory tract evolved to continually clear itself of dust, campfire smudge, and pollen, we encounter asthma and allergies when they are missing. Our immune systems are designed to be challenged.

For those with allergies, a cure may not be far off. Understanding how our immune systems become misdirected is leading to new attempts to refocus them on more appropriate targets. The ultimate treatment will be to re-

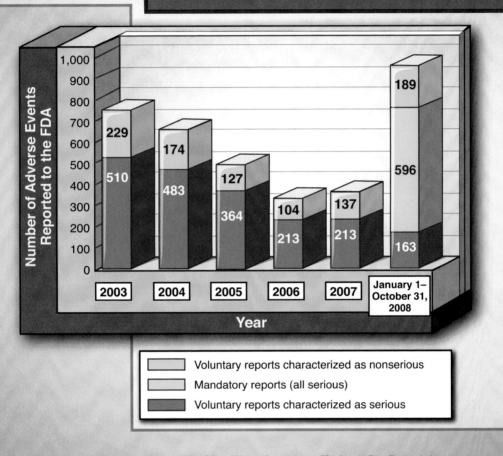

Adverse Events Related to Dietary Supplements

Number of Adverse Events Reported to the FDA

- 2003: 229, 510
- 2004: 174, 483
- 2005: 127, 364
- 2006: 104, 213
- 2007: 137, 213
- January 1–October 31, 2008: 189, 596, 163

Year

Legend:
- Voluntary reports characterized as nonserious
- Mandatory reports (all serious)
- Voluntary reports characterized as serious

Taken from: Government Accountability Office, "Dietary Supplements: FDA Should Take Further Actions to Improve Oversight and Consumer Understanding," January 2009.

open the window of tolerance that exists after birth, reestablishing our original connection to the natural world. This great hope for allergy sufferers will be filled not by drug companies marketing their latest me-too antihistamine but by basic scientists in university laboratories.

Evolutionary-minded researchers are now finding that it may be best to feed infants peanuts and other potential food allergens in infancy in order to avoid allergies later. And for autoimmunity sufferers, rest assured you won't have to swallow worms for a cure. Researchers are already at work extracting the specific chemicals used by parasites to suppress our immune systems.

Even before this research is done, an evolutionary perspective points to a more natural way to prevent allergies and autoimmune conditions. We can expose ourselves to the myriad challenges and benefits of living in a world of dirt and flowers and trees and animals. Instead of overprotecting our children and thereby putting them at risk, we need to put them in nature's way.

CHAPTER 3

Personal Narratives About Autoimmune Diseases

Those with Autoimmune Diseases Should Not Have to Suffer in Silence

Lauren Del Vecchio

In the following viewpoint Lauren Del Vecchio talks about the heart-break of having an autoimmune disease. According to Del Vecchio, confusion and shame were her frequent companions for years after she received a diagnosis of scleroderma and mixed connective tissue disease at the age of nineteen. However, when she learned the disease was destroying her heart, she felt compelled to share her story in order to spread awareness about autoimmune diseases. Del Vecchio lives in New York City and blogs about her condition at http://savelaurensheart.com. In October 2007, at age twenty-five, she learned that her heart was covered in scar tissue and was failing. She now lives with a pacemaker/defibrillator implanted in her chest.

Photo on previous page. A patient afflicted with the autoimmune disease lupus suffers from the skin lesions that are symptomatic of the disease. (Scott Camazine/Photo Researchers, Inc.)

I started writing here with one goal on my mind: raise awareness for autoimmune disease. This is a story I've never shared before except with those very close to me but I feel compelled to write about it now in the spirit of spreading awareness during this month [March;

SOURCE: Lauren Del Vecchio, "Misconceptions of Autoimmune Disease—a Story About Heartbreak," savelaurensheart.com, March 15, 2010. Reproduced by permission.

National Autoimmune Disease Awareness Month] that has been dedicated to doing so.

I was diagnosed with Scleroderma/Mixed Connective Tissue Disease in Spring 2001 at 19 years old after many years of doctors visits with different symptoms. I was very confused and scared and I knew by the look on my mom's face this wasn't good. What she had learned was heartbreaking enough for a mother. The two words I noticed to be associated with Scleroderma in whatever I read about it at that point were "incurable" and "fatal."

I shared the news with my family and close friends who shared my confusion and we did our best to make sense of it with the little knowledge we had and the little information available at the time. I turned to my then boyfriend and, looking for comfort, I told him what I had just learned. The very first thing he said to me was "What? I can't catch this, can I?" My heart sunk down to my toes and broke to pieces. Needless to say, he wasn't my boyfriend for much longer after that. But that one sentence changed me forever in an instant.

> **FAST FACT**
>
> According to the Lupus Foundation of America, heart disease is a major complication of lupus and a leading cause of death among people living with autoimmune disease.

A Secret I Had to Keep

From that point on I kept it to myself. Anyone I would meet in college, all the boys I liked and went out with or wanted to get to know . . . I wouldn't ever DREAM of trying to explain something like this to them. It felt like a secret I had to keep. How do you begin to explain something so complex to someone? I even had to explain it to nurses at the time because that's how rare it was nine years ago. It would have been easier to just say "I have cancer" because then people just get it, nod their heads, and understand they cannot "catch it." I put up a wall and promised I wouldn't ever put myself in a position to feel that awful ever again so I rarely told anyone about my condition.

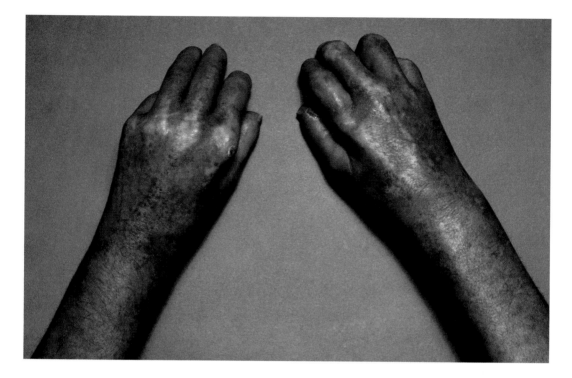

This person suffers from the shiny, toughened skin on the hands typical in scleroderma patients. Scleroderma is an autoimmune disease in which the body's immune system attacks its own cells, resulting in hardening of the body's connective tissues. (SPL/Photo Researchers, Inc.)

I lived my life and it was easy to pretend I was fine with limited bad days, a busy schedule, and I was on meds (methotrexate—which, in large doses is chemotherapy) that supposedly had me in remission. Little did I know that one day it would ravage my body and set sights on my heart, changing my life forever once again.

During that period and in the years since I have even gotten a handful of people that hear "autoimmune disease" and immediately stop listening—and I guess upon hearing the word "immune" they go "Oh, like AIDS?!" Well, NO it is nothing like HIV or AIDS. You cannot acquire an autoimmune disease through contact, or "catch it" that way either. You are born with a predisposition to it. It is in your DNA. It is your body's failure to regulate one or many of its systems. In my case, it is overproduction of collagen (scar tissue) and a disease of the small blood vessels. My body cannot regulate its healing reactions and it goes into overdrive and attacks not only the germs but its own organs (i.e: the case with my heart).

Time to Share My Story

I got many surprise reactions from many people when I was told my heart was failing in 2007. They had no idea where it came from. I always seemed fine, like nothing was wrong, and it even caught me by surprise. But I had kept my autoimmune disease a secret for so long that it was time to share my story and spread the word. If I can help even one woman or teenage girl avoid the confusion and unreasonable shame I felt then I feel I have done something good. No boyfriend should ever ask this question of their girl ever again.

In a world where autoimmune disease affects 1 in every 13 women it's quite impossible to believe that 90% of people cannot name a single autoimmune disease.

Let's please change this. The more we know, the more research gets done, the more of a chance we find cures and ways to manage these terrible diseases. Or even better, prevent them.

These days I have a man who loves me and my scarred heart to the end of time. He's got my back in this quest to heal myself and change the game in autoimmune diseases awareness.

I would love your help in doing so as well.

A Witness to the Havoc of Autoimmune Diseases

Kellie Martin

In the following viewpoint Kellie Martin shares the story of her sister's swift and untimely death from lupus. According to Martin, lupus struck her nineteen-year-old sister without warning. Doctors originally misdiagnosed the disease, and this allowed lupus to wreak havoc on her organs and cause her death. Martin is an American television actress. Since her sister's death she has become a spokesperson for the American Autoimmune Related Diseases Association.

I'm a sister, a daughter, a stepdaughter, a wife, a potential mother, an actress, a woman and a friend. But most of all, I'm a witness to the havoc autoimmune diseases wreak on those they strike, the devastation they level on families and loved ones, and the terrible price we pay for one of the biggest problems associated with autoimmune diseases . . . getting a correct diagnosis in a reasonable amount of time before major damage is done.

SOURCE: Kellie Martin, "A Witness," in *The Savvy Woman Patient: How and Why Your Sex Matters to Your Health,* Jennifer Wider and Phyllis Greenberger, eds. Copyright © 2006 Capital Books. Reproduced by permission of Kellie Martin.

I'm a witness to my sister, Heather. Heather and I were always best friends. For 19 years, I watched my little sister grow into a beautiful woman. I was there when she was born, and I was there when she died.

A few days after finishing her sophomore year at college, Heather couldn't get out of bed. The doctor said it was the flu. This doctor was new to my family. He'd never had to handle anything more than a sore throat for us.

When Heather's abdominal pain, fever, nausea, and insomnia got worse, the doctor prescribed an anti-nausea medication. She had a violent allergic reaction to it. She started to convulse. She lost control of her neck muscles, and her eyes rolled back in her head.

That was Heather's first visit to the emergency room, but she was treated only for the convulsions. They didn't deal with anything else . . . her stiff joints, intense muscle pain, fatigue, her inability to eat. She was so weak, she couldn't hold a spoon. Later, she couldn't eat because she had sores in her mouth, and it hurt her too much.

The following night, Heather had to go back to the emergency room for abdominal pain and horrible cramping in her legs. They gave her a painkiller and sent her home. The next day, my mom had to take her back again. They went to the emergency room three times in three days. Then they finally put Heather in the hospital. My mother had to beg the doctor to admit her.

At the hospital, the nurses took blood from Heather three times a day, and each day, a new specialist was called in to see her . . . an internist, an infectious-disease specialist, a hematologist [a specialist in blood and bone marrow diseases]. As a last resort, they gave Heather a test for lupus. But they still thought Heather had an unusual virus, so the doctors discharged her.

> **FAST FACT**
>
> Autoimmune disease is one of the top ten leading causes of death in female children and adults in all age groups up to sixty-four years of age, according to the American Autoimmune Related Diseases Association.

My mom and I carried Heather into the house and put her in bed. We knew she'd feel better in her own room with her dog, Sparky. She was relieved to be home, but she got weaker every day. It seemed like she was sent home, not to get better, but because no one knew how to help an incapacitated 19-year-old who had been completely healthy two weeks earlier.

The doctor told us he believed that Heather had a virus that was attacking her joints and muscles. My mom asked if the results had come back from the lupus panel. The doctor said that he'd gotten a verbal response that the test was negative. He told us to go home and put a cool cloth on Heather's forehead for her fever. He smiled, patted her on the head and left.

That night, for the first time in her life, Heather crawled into bed with our mother. That was highly unusual; Heather wasn't afraid of anything. She was much more like a big sister, even though I'm three years older. Heather was the rock of our family.

Lupus Ravaged My Sister's Body

We took Heather to another doctor's office, where her condition was diagnosed two minutes after her examination. The doctor looked really disturbed when he saw Heather's hospital charts and medical history. He ordered a second lupus panel because the first one never appeared in her file. The next day, Heather was admitted to the hospital because of dehydration and kidney failure—both caused by lupus.

We were given a list of treatments that Heather would be getting: steroids, vitamins, fluids. During her first week at the hospital, the blood vessels in Heather's lungs began to burst. Her breathing became more labored. The doctors also found that the lupus had affected Heather's liver and bone marrow. The list of treatments increased to antibiotics and chemotherapy.

Lupus attacks multiple systems in the body that may include the skin, joints, lungs, blood, blood vessels, heart, kidneys, liver, brain, and nervous system. (John M. Daughherty/Photo Researchers, Inc.)

Heather liked to be in control, and while her body was so out of control, she wanted to make decisions . . . even though she knew she had no choice. When they said she had to go into the intensive-care unit [ICU], it was her choice to go in. But, after that, nothing was her decision, because she was sedated from then on and her body started its descent.

The night before Heather went into ICU, though, she had an amazing burst of energy. It was exactly like the old Heather. She didn't want to rest, she wanted to talk . . . about school, basketball, friends, boyfriends, everything. She sang songs, talked on the phone. That night was such a gift.

I'm still trying to make sense of what happened to Heather. Because of her experience, I've gotten sort of a crash course in lupus and autoimmune disease. I've learned that my stepmother also has lupus, and that one of my best friends from college has just been diagnosed with scleroderma. Those are very close relations in my life.

You may think autoimmune disease hasn't touched your family. I'll bet that all you have to do is scratch the surface, and you'll find it has.

Until we can find a cure for autoimmune diseases, I'm told our best hope is early, prompt diagnosis. Something my sister was not fortunate enough to receive. But, something that is well within our reach.

Our Autoimmune Diseases Brought Us Together

Trudie Mitschang, interview with John Crawford and Debbie Crawford

In the following viewpoint Trudie Mitschang from the magazine *IG Living!* interviews John and Debbie Crawford. The couple both have a rare autoimmune disease called stiff person syndrome (SPS). They met and began sharing their lives together after John, newly diagnosed, found a story about SPS that Debbie had posted on the Internet. The couple tells Mitschang that despite their diseases, they try to live life to the fullest. Mitschang is a writer for *IG Living!*, a magazine for those who depend on immune globulin (IG) treatments to fight their diseases.

In this issue, we chat with John Crawford, 65, and Debbie Crawford, 52, who both suffer from stiff person syndrome (SPS), a rare disorder affecting only one in one million people. Prior to the advent of the Internet, the odds of John and Debbie meeting, much less falling in love, were on par with contracting the disease—one in a million. But thanks to technology, John and

SOURCE: Trudie Mitschang, "Let's Talk!," *IG Living!*, February/March 2010. Reproduced by permission.

Debbie will celebrate their second wedding anniversary this year. Their story will be featured in the latest edition of the popular *Chicken Soup for the Soul* series titled "*True Love.*" In the story "Go For It," Debbie shares her thoughts about how to be disabled without letting disability define you.

Trudie Mitschang: What are the symptoms of SPS and how is it treated?

John Crawford: SPS is a rare disease of the nervous system. The symptoms include progressively severe muscle stiffness in the spine and lower extremities and painful episodic muscle spasms that can come on suddenly. Most people with SPS have other autoimmune disorders as well.

Debbie Crawford: There are variances in the symptoms of SPS. Treatments include intravenous immune globulin (IVIG) and plasmapheresis, as well as pharmacological therapy. Some also may benefit from behavioral and physical therapy.

Tell me how the two of you met.

John: I was widowed shortly after I was diagnosed with SPS; doctors had given me two years to live. I began treatment with IVIG and miraculously began to get better. I met Debbie when I was searching online for support groups and came across her website. Her story moved me and I sent her an email with my phone number. A few weeks later, she contacted me and we became very close friends.

Debbie: When I met John, we had an instant rapport and shared a lot of things besides our SPS—it wasn't just commiserating and complaining. We have a similar "gallows" sense of humor, and we were friends for four years before finally meeting face to face in August 2007. My previous marriage had failed, and I was cautious about a new relationship. Plus, we really had to come to terms with the fact that both of us having SPS could be a tremendous challenge; we didn't want to be a burden to one another.

Caring for Each Other and Making the Most of Every Moment

Since both of you have chronic illnesses, who is the caregiver in your relationship?

John: We take turns. In addition to SPS, Debbie is a type 1 diabetic and I have chronic inflammatory polyneuropathy (CIDP). I also have heart problems, so we don't know what the future holds. But we are committed to making the most of every moment.

Debbie: Between the two of us, our calendar is peppered with doctors' appointments, which we turn into lunch dates! I help him button his shirt, and he helps me put on my pantyhose; so it's give and take all the way. With our combined ailments, we buy our medications in bulk, and then there's all of our medical equipment, gait aids and handicapped placards. We understand our reality and limitations, but our motto is: "The only future is the day." We make the most of each one.

SPS can be very debilitating. Tell me about some of the issues and how you have overcome them.

> **FAST FACT**
>
> According to a 2001 survey by the American Autoimmune Related Diseases Association, over 45 percent of patients with autoimmune diseases have been labeled as chronic complainers in the earliest stages of their illness.

John: People look at us and assume we are so in love because we are always holding hands. The truth is: We are holding each other up!

Debbie: Fear of open spaces is a common concern. With SPS, your muscles can just lock up unexpectedly, which can be terrifying if you are crossing a busy intersection or riding an escalator. For me, it was a matter of facing the issues head on.

How do you pay it forward?

John: I always look for opportunities to help others. We're very involved in our church, and we have a nursing home ministry where we visit the seniors once a month.

Debbie: I pay it forward through my website outreach with information, a personal perspective and hope. I love to post silly pages that make people laugh. Sharing a smile with others is such an easy thing to do, but it can make a huge difference in someone's day.

You both have a great sense of humor. What makes you laugh?

John: SPS is a bizarre syndrome. Finding humor in some of my quirky situations is a positive way I cope. Laughing at yourself helps you become better, not bitter.

Debbie: I find humor in children and reality. Like John, I look for the laughter instead of tears with my SPS. We find humor in each other.

How has IVIG helped you?

John: I'm just starting with IVIG again, and it's been a tremendous help to me. Now I am able to walk around the block.

Debbie: IVIG has helped us tremendously. Even though it's not a cure, it can really improve your quality of life and should be available to anyone who needs it.

What are you looking forward to?

John: Loving Debbie as long as I can. I never dreamed I would remarry, so I'm very fortunate. One thing I said many years ago is it's not what kills you that amazes me, but it's what you can live with and still survive. Here I am with five illnesses and able to do as much as I do; Debbie has made me a stronger, more vital human being.

Debbie: I want as blessed and full a future as I can have. I have been encouraged to write. I want to enjoy my children and grandchildren. John and I know our lifetime is just a season. We choose to make it Christmas.

GLOSSARY

adaptive immunity   A type of immune response found only in vertebrate animals that is specific and long lived and is based on "immunological memory." Adaptive immunity involves the production of antibodies that are specific to each antigen.

Addison's disease   A potentially fatal autoimmune disease involving the destruction of cells in the adrenal cortex (the gland that sits above the kidneys and mediates stress responses).

antibody   A protein (immunoglobulin) produced by B cells that is involved in the adaptive immune response. Specific antibodies are produced in response to each different antigen.

antigen   Any substance, molecule, cell, or microbe that the immune system recognizes and that can stimulate an immune response.

antioxidant   A molecule that prevents oxidation. In the body, antioxidants attach to other molecules called free radicals and prevent the free radicals from causing damage to cell walls, DNA, and other parts of the cell. Vitamin E, vitamin C, and beta carotene are common antioxidants.

autoantibody   An antibody produced in the body that attacks its own cells, tissues, and/or organs.

autoimmunity   A condition in which the body's immune system produces antibodies in response to its own tissues or blood components instead of to foreign particles or microorganisms.

B cells (B lymphocytes)   The immune cells, or white blood cells, that are responsible for producing antibodies.

basophil   A white blood cell that releases histamine (a substance involved in allergic reactions) and that produces substances to attract other white blood cells (neutrophils and eosinophils) to a trouble spot.

Crohn's disease	An autoimmune disease in which immune cells attack cells of the gastrointestinal tract, causing abdominal pain and diarrhea.
cytokines	Proteins secreted by cells that act as the immune system's messengers and that help regulate an immune response.
dendritic cell	A cell that is derived from white blood cells, resides in tissues, and helps T cells recognize foreign antigens.
diabetes	*See* **type 1 diabetes; type 2 diabetes.**
eosinophil	A white blood cell that kills bacteria and other foreign cells.
Graves' disease	An autoimmune disease that causes the thyroid to make too much thyroid hormone.
Guillain-Barré syndrome	An autoimmune disease system where immune cells attack part of the nervous system, causing muscle weakness and paralysis.
Hashimoto's thyroiditis	An autoimmune disease involving gradual destruction of the thyroid gland and an underproduction of thyroid hormone.
helper T cell	A white blood cell that helps other immune cells do their job. For instance, helper T cells help B cells recognize and produce antibodies against foreign antigens and help killer T cells become active.
immune response	The physiological response of the body, controlled by the immune system, that fights off specific foreign substances or agents (antigens).
immune system	The defense mechanisms of the body that protect it against foreign substances and organisms causing infection. Humans have both innate and adaptive immune systems.
immune tolerance	The natural safeguards that the immune system possesses that protect it from harming its own cells and tissues. Defects in immune tolerance lead to autoimmunity.
immunoglobulin (Ig)	A protein produced by B cells that is involved in the adaptive immune response. Also called an antibody. Specific immuno-

globulins are produced in response to each antigen the body encounters. Immunoglobulins are divided into five classes: IgA, IgD, IgE, IgG, and IgM.

immunosuppressant Any chemical or substance that suppresses the immune response of an individual. For instance, the chemical cyclosporine is typically given after organ transplant surgery to prevent the immune system from attacking the new organ.

innate immunity An ancient immune response based on a general, nonspecific detection of foreign substances.

killer T cell A T cell that attaches to foreign or abnormal cells and kills them.

leukocytes The cells of the immune system, also called white blood cells.

lupus A chronic, multisystem autoimmune disorder. It can affect the joints, skin, kidneys, lungs, heart, or brain.

lymphatic system A part of the immune system, the lymphatic system is composed of a network of vessels and nodes that transports lymph fluid containing antibodies and white blood cells and that filters out foreign invaders.

lymphocyte A type of immune cell, or white blood cell. There are three major types of lymphocytes: B cells, T cells, and natural killer cells.

macrophage A type of immune cell, or white blood cell, that ingests bacteria and other foreign substances.

major histo-compatibility complex (MHC) An area of the genome that codes for a series of proteins expressed on the surface of cells. These proteins serve as markers that allow the immune system to distinguish between "self" proteins, which belong in the body, and "nonself" proteins, which are foreign.

major histo-compatibility complex (MHC) molecules Proteins found on cell surfaces that help the immune system to distinguish between "self" and "nonself" cells.

mast cell	A cell in tissues that releases histamine and other substances involved in inflammatory and allergic reactions.
microorganism	An organism, such as bacteria, protozoa, and some fungi, that can be seen only through a microscope.
multiple sclerosis	A disease in which the immune system attacks the protective coating around the nerves. The damage affects the brain and spinal cord.
myasthenia gravis	An autoimmune disorder involving the destruction of the neurotransmitter acetylcholine, resulting in muscle weakness.
natural killer cell	A type of white blood cell that is naturally able to kill abnormal cells, (that is, it does not have to learn that the cells are abnormal). Natural killer cells are components of the innate immune system in humans.
paresthesia	A prickly, tingling, or burning sensation on the skin.
passive immunity	Immunity conferred by antibodies that are produced in a body other than one's own. Infants have passive immunity because they are born with antibodies that are transferred through the placenta from the mother. These antibodies disappear between six and twelve months of age.
pathogen	A disease-causing microorganism.
phagocyte	A cell, similar to a macrophage, that ingests and destroys invading microorganisms, other cells, and cell fragments.
receptor	A molecule on a cell's surface or inside the cell that allows only molecules that fit precisely in it—as a key fits in its lock—to attach to it.
regulatory (suppressor) T cell	A white blood cell that helps end an immune response.
rheumatoid arthritis	An autoimmune disease in which the immune system attacks the lining of the joints throughout the body.
scleroderma	An autoimmune disease causing abnormal growth of connective tissue in the skin and blood vessels.

Sjögren's syndrome	An autoimmune disease targeting moisture-producing glands and causing dryness in the mouth and eyes. Other parts of the body—the stomach, pancreas, intestines, and ovaries—can be affected as well.
T cell	A type of lymphocyte, or white blood cell, involved in adaptive immunity. Different types of T cells help to orchestrate the immune response.
thymus	An organ that is part of the lymphatic system and in which T cells grow and multiply. It is located in the chest behind the breastbone.
type 1 diabetes	An autoimmune disease, also called juvenile diabetes, in which the immune system attacks the cells that make insulin, a hormone needed to control blood sugar levels.
type 2 diabetes	A disease caused primarily when the body's cells become resistant to insulin, causing uncontrolled blood sugar levels. Some researchers have suggested that type 2 diabetes may be caused by an autoimmune disorder involving the innate immune system.

CHRONOLOGY

1875   Karl Weigert detects bacteria in humans for the first time.

1884–1887   Russian scientist Élie Metchnikoff, considered one of the fathers of immunology, observes that phagocytes within starfish envelope and digest foreign bodies, including bacteria.

1890   Emil von Behring develops serum therapy (the treatment of disease by administration of a serum obtained from an immunized animal) for diphtheria (along with Erich Wernicke) and tetanus (along with Shibasaburo Kitasato).

1892   Polish scientist Paul Ehrlich, also considered one of the fathers of immunology, demonstrates the passive transfer of antibodies from mother to fetus across the placenta and from mother to newborn via breast milk.

1900   Ehrlich and his student Julius Morganroth publish the doctrine of horror autotoxicus, which holds that autoimmunity cannot occur because it would be incompatible with life.

1903–1908   Clemens von Pirquet suggests that the symptoms of diseases like measles, which appear about a week after infection, are not ending because of the immune response, but are actually initiated by immune response. Pirquet says famously, "The conception that antibodies, which should protect against disease, are also responsible for disease, sounds at first absurd."

1904   Julius Donath and Karl Landsteiner demonstrate that paroxysmal cold hemoglobinuria (PKH) is an autoimmune disease.

1910   Pirquet and Bela Schick publish the book *Allergie* and coin the term *allergy* to describe altered reactivity in which the immune response itself causes clinical disease.

1940   Erik Waaler discovers the antibody known as the "rheumatoid factor," which is present in the blood of people with rheumatoid arthritis.

1944   Peter Medawar develops a hypothesis of allograft rejection.

1945   Robert Royston Coombs shows that many causes of acquired hemolytic anemia are due to "incomplete" antibodies.

1948   Malcolm Hargraves discovers a substance he calls the lupus factor in the nucleus of people with lupus erythematosus.

1954   Peter Miescher shows that the lupus factor described by Hargraves is an autoantibody to the cell nucleus.

1956   Noel R. Rose and Ernst Witebsky provide proof of an autoimmune disease affecting the thyroid gland.

1956–1957   Deborah Doniach and Ivan Roitt publish a series of articles describing autoimmunity as the cause of Hashimoto's thyroiditis.

1957   Noel R. Rose and Ernst Witebsky publish the Witebsky postulates to establish the etiology of an autoimmune disease.

1957 Immunologist Frank Macfarlane Burnet develops the clonal-selection theory of antibody diversity.

1960 Burnet and Medawar receive the 1960 Nobel Prize in Physiology or Medicine for demonstrating the concept of acquired immune tolerance.

1963 The first textbooks on immunology are published: *Clinical Aspects of Immunology* by Philip George H. Gell and Robert Royston Coombs, and *Immunology for Students of Medicine* by J.H. Humphrey and R.G. White.

1970 Richard Gershon and Kazunari Kondo discover suppressor T cells.

Early 1970s Rolf Kiessling discovers natural killer cells.

1971 Cyclosporin, the first immunosuppressive drug that selectively suppresses T cells, is discovered.

Late 1970s Susumu Tonegawa demonstrates how B cells produce a vast array of antibodies using what is called VDJ recombination.

1993 Rose revises and updates the Witebsky postulates.

1995–2003 Shimon Sakaguchi discovers regulatory T cells and Foxp3, the gene directing their development.

2000–2005 Trevor Marshall develops an alternative theory for the cause of many autoimmune diseases.

ORGANIZATIONS TO CONTACT

The editors have compiled the following list of organizations concerned with the issues debated in this book. The descriptions are derived from materials provided by the organizations. All have publications or information available for interested readers. The list was compiled on the date of publication of the present volume; the information provided here may change. Be aware that many organizations take several weeks or longer to respond to inquiries, so allow as much time as possible.

American Autoimmune Related Diseases Association (AARDA)
22100 Gratiot Ave.
East Detroit, MI 48021
phone: (586) 776-3900
fax: (586) 776-3903
e-mail: www.aarda.org/formemail/dd-form mailer.php
website: www.aarda.org

The AARDA is a nonprofit organization dedicated to bringing a national focus to autoimmunity and eradicating autoimmune diseases. The AARDA seeks to increase knowledge of autoimmune diseases and foster collaboration in the areas of education, public awareness, research, and patient services in an effective, ethical, and efficient manner. The association publishes *Infocus*, a newsletter. The AARDA forum at www.aarda.org/forum2 is an active online community for those concerned about autoimmune diseases.

Arthritis Foundation
PO Box 7669
Atlanta, GA 30357-0669
phone: (800) 283-7800
website: www.arthritis.org

The Arthritis Foundation is a national nonprofit organization that supports the more than one hundred types of arthritis and related conditions. The Arthritis Foundation is one of the largest private nonprofit contributors to arthritis research in the world. The foundation helps people take control of arthritis by providing public health education, pursuing public policy and legislation, and conducting evidence-based programs to improve the quality of life for those living with arthritis. The Arthritis Foundation publishes *Arthritis Today* magazine, which offers information and tools to help people with arthritis live a better life.

Autoimmunity Research Foundation (ARF)
3423 Hill Canyon Ave.
Thousand Oaks, CA 91360
phone: (818) 584-1201
website: http://auto immunityresearch.org

The ARF is a nonprofit organization devoted to advancing new and effective therapies to treat autoimmune diseases. The organization focuses on the work of Trevor Marshall, who devises treatments for autoimmune diseases based on the view that they are all chronic inflammatory diseases. The ARF website provides information about the model of autoimmune diseases as chronic inflammatory diseases and on the Marshall Protocol advocated by the organization to treat autoimmune diseases.

Immune Disease Institute (IDI)
3 Blackfan Cir., 3rd Fl.
Boston, MA 02115
phone: (617) 713-8000
website: www.idi.har vard.edu

The IDI is a nonprofit corporation affliated with Children's Hospital Boston and Harvard Medical School. The mission of the IDI is to carry out fundamental biomedical research in immunology and autoimmunity in order to improve human health, harness inflammation, and strengthen immune defense. Each year the IDI holds several seminars and other events to inform the public about its research milestones. The IDI's annual report gives an accounting of the organization's contributions and how its biomedical breakthroughs are benefiting the lives of patients with serious and often fatal diseases.

Lupus Foundation of America (LFA)
2000 L St. NW, Ste. 710
Washington, DC 20036
phone: (202) 349-1155
fax: (202) 349-1156
website: www.lupus.org

The LFA is a national nonprofit voluntary health organization dedicated to finding the causes of and cure for lupus and to providing support, services, and hope to all people affected by lupus. The LFA pursues its mission by providing research funding, advocating for increased public and private sector support for research on lupus, providing information to and supporting those affected by lupus, and heightening public awareness about the disease. The organization's magazine, *Lupus Now*, is published three times each year and includes lifestyle and wellness feature articles, the latest news in research and treatments, clinical updates, and personal stories.

National Institute of Allergy and Infectious Diseases (NIAID)
Office of Communications and Government Relations
6610 Rockledge Dr.
MSC 6612
Bethesda, MD 20892
phone: (301) 402-1663
fax: (301) 402-0120
e-mail: niaidnews@niaid.nih.gov
website: www.niaid.nih.gov

The NIAID is one of the twenty-seven institutes and centers of the National Institutes of Health. The NIAID conducts and supports basic and applied research to better understand, treat, and ultimately prevent infectious, immunologic, and allergic diseases. The NIAID provides several pamphlets and fact sheets and conducts seminars and conferences on immune diseases.

National Institute of Arthritis and Musculoskeletal and Skin Diseases (NIAMS)
Information Clearinghouse/NIH
1 AMS Cir.
Bethesda, MD 20892
phone: (301) 495-4484
website: www.nih.gov/niams/healthinfo

The NIAMS is one of the twenty-seven institutes and centers of the National Institutes of Health. The mission of the NIAMS is to support research into the causes, treatment, and prevention of arthritis and musculoskeletal and skin diseases; the training of basic and clinical scientists to carry out this research; and the dissemination of information on research progress in these diseases. The NIAMS multimedia page provides access to videos, images, and audio publications.

National Organization for Rare Disorders (NORD)
55 Kenosia Ave.
PO Box 1968
Danbury, CT
06813-1968
phone: (203) 744-0100
fax: (203) 798-2291
e-mail: orphan@rarediseases.org
website: www.rarediseases.org

NORD is a nonprofit organization composed of voluntary health organizations dedicated to helping people with rare "orphan" diseases and assisting the organizations that serve them. NORD is committed to the identification, treatment, and cure of rare disorders through programs of education, advocacy, research, and service. The organization publishes books and guides such as the *NORD Resource Guide*, where families can find sources of help and encouragement; and the *NORD Guide to Rare Disorders*, a textbook for physicians and health-care providers. The *Orphan Disease Update* is a newsletter published by NORD three times per year.

Scleroderma Foundation
300 Rosewood Dr.
Ste. 105
Danvers, MA 01923
phone: (800) 722-4673
fax: (978) 463-5809
e-mail: sfinfo@sclero
derma.org
website: www.sclero
derma.org

The Scleroderma Foundation is a nonprofit organization devoted to educating the public about scleroderma, supporting those who have scleroderma, and funding research with the goal of finding a cure for scleroderma. To promote education about the disease, the foundation facilitates health and professional seminars, produces and distributes literature, and conducts publicity campaigns. To help support the three hundred thousand people living with scleroderma, the foundation offers peer counseling, mutual support programs, and physician referrals. To support research into a cure for scleroderma, the foundation donates $1 million on average each year. The foundation publishes a magazine, *Scleroderma Voice*, and provides medical brochures and other print publications.

Sjögren's Syndrome Foundation
6707 Democracy Blvd.
Ste. 325
Bethesda, MD 20817
phone: (800) 475-6473
fax: (301) 530-4415
e-mail: tms@sjogrens
.org
website: www.sjogrens
.org

The Sjögren's Syndrome Foundation is a nonprofit national voluntary health agency that provides patients with practical information and coping strategies that minimize the effects of Sjögren's syndrome. In addition, the foundation is the clearinghouse for medical information and is the recognized national advocate for Sjögren's syndrome. The foundation's mission is to educate patients and their families about Sjögren's syndrome, increase public and professional awareness of Sjögren's syndrome, and encourage research into new treatments and a cure. The foundation publishes a newsletter called the *Moisture Seekers*, as well as several brochures and fact sheets.

FOR FURTHER READING

Books

Rita Baron-Faust and Jill P. Buyon, *The Autoimmune Connection*. New York: McGraw Hill, 2004.

Kyle J. Brenner, *Autoimmune Diseases: Symptoms, Diagnosis, and Treatment*. Hauppauge, NY: Nova Science, 2010.

Art Brownstein, *Extraordinary Healing*. Gig Harbor, WA: Harbor, 2005.

Caroline Cox, *The Fight to Survive: A Young Girl, Diabetes, and the Discovery of Insulin*. New York: Kaplan, 2009.

Barbara Giesser, *Primer on Multiple Sclerosis*. New York: Oxford University Press, 2011.

Dan Hurley, *Diabetes Rising: How a Rare Disease Became a Modern Pandemic, and What to Do About It*. New York: Kaplan, 2010.

Robert G. Lahita and Ina L. Yalof, *Women and Autoimmune Disease: The Mysterious Ways Your Body Betrays Itself*. New York: William Morrow, 2004.

Tak W. Mak and Mary Saunders, *Primer to the Immune Response*. Boston: Academic, 2008.

Elaine Moore, *Autoimmune Diseases and Their Environmental Triggers*. Jefferson, NC: McFarland, 2002.

Gunter Müller, *New Immunology Research Developments*. New York: Nova Science, 2009.

Donna Jackson Nakazawa, *The Autoimmune Epidemic: Bodies Gone Haywire in a World Out of Balance—and the Cutting-Edge Science that Promises Hope*. New York: Simon & Schuster, 2008.

Duane O'Mahony and Anrai de Burca, eds., *Women and Multiple Sclerosis*. New York: Nova Biomedical, 2010.

Noel R. Rose and Ian R. Mackay, eds., *The Autoimmune Diseases*. 4th ed. New York: Academic, 2006.

Michael Sticherling and Enno Christophers, eds., *Treatment of Autoimmune Disorders*. New York: Springer, 2003.

Michael H. Weisman, *Rheumatoid Arthritis.* New York: Oxford University Press, 2011.

Periodicals

Karen Barrow, "A 'Forest Fire of Hair Loss,' and Its Scars," *New York Times,* July 5, 2010.

Katherine Bowers, "New Hope for Millions," *Self,* June 2010.

Rachel Caspi, "Immunotherapy of Autoimmunity and Cancer: The Penalty for Success," *Nature Reviews Immunology,* December 8, 2008.

Elaine Freeman, "High Time for Hi Cy?," *Hopkins Medicine,* Winter 2008.

Linda Geddes, "Autoimmune Disease Cells Harnessed to Fight Cancer," *New Scientist,* October 2009.

John Ioannidis, "Why Most Published Research Findings Are False," *PLoS Medicine,* August 30, 2005.

Anita Manning, "Mysteries of Autoimmune Diseases Unravel," *USA Today,* September 3, 2007.

Dennis McGonagle and Michael F. McDermott, "A Proposed Classification of the Immunological Diseases," *PLoS Medicine,* 2006.

Stephanie Pappas, "The Yin-Yang Factor: It Could Wreck Your Immune System, or Save Your Life," *Stanford Medicine,* Fall 2009.

Andrew Pollack, "Trying to Shut Off the Body's Friendly Fire," *New York Times,* June 5, 2005.

Janet Raloff, "Counting Side Effects," *Science News,* November 2, 2009.

Noel Rose, "Life Amidst the Contrivances," *Nature Immunology,* October 10, 2006.

Science Daily, "Important Control Mechanism Behind Autoimmune Diseases Discovered," May 4, 2010.

Emily Singer, "The New Hygiene Hypothesis," *Technology Review,* January 3, 2008.

Liz Szabo, "Autism Tied to Autoimmune Diseases in Immediate Family," *USA Today,* August 10, 2010.

Amy Wallace, "An Epidemic of Fear: How Panicked Parents Skipping Shots Endangers Us All," *Wired,* October 19, 2009.

INDEX

A

Addison's disease, 27
Allergies, 45–46, 104
  antigens triggering, 33
  autoimmune disease *vs.*, 75
  hygiene hypothesis and, 77–79
  prevalence of, 74
  prevention of, 111–112
AlterNet (website), 81
American Autoimmune Related Diseases
  Association, 13, 45, 46, 53, 119
Amyotrophic lateral sclerosis (Lou
  Gehrig's disease), 19
  symptoms of, 26
Anemia. *See* Autoimmune hemolytic
  anemia; Pernicious anemia
Ankylosing spondylitis, 19, 62
  symptoms of, 26
Antibodies, 23, 105
  IgG class, 28
  types of, 37
Antigens, 18, 33
  immune cells' response to, 36–40
  See also Human leukocyte antigen
Arshad, Syed Hasan, 75
Autoantibodies, 19, 30, 107
Autoimmune diseases
  affect more women than men, 57–63
  affecting organs/organ systems, *20*
  autoimmunity *vs.*, 43
  clusters of, 87–89
  common symptoms shared by, 23–27
  difficulty in diagnosis of, 27–28, 62,
    82–83

  factors in triggering, 23, 46–47
  gender differences in incidents of, by
    disorder, *61*
  gender disparity in, 17
  genes play key role in, 52–56
  genetic basis of, 48–51, 52–56
  hygiene hypothesis can explain rise in,
    73–80
  number of genetic variants identified for,
    by disorder, *54*
  prevalence of, 16, 58, 60, 82
  role of vitamin D in prevention of, is not
    certain, 94–101
  types of, 19, 21–22
  vaccines play role in causing, 90–93
Autoimmune hemolytic anemia, 19
  symptoms of, 25
Autoimmune thrombocytic purpura, 19
  symptoms of, 25
Autoimmunity, 17
  autoimmune disease *vs.*, 43
  causes of, 43–44
  triggers of, 23

B

B cells, 10, 12, *15*, 34, 36–37
  destruction of, in type 1 diabetes, *69*
Bach, Jean-Francois, 77
Barrel effect, 86–87
Basophils, 40
Behe, Michael, 13
BioEssays (journal), 68, 97
Bone marrow, 34
Burks, Wesley, 79